GW00320368

THANK GOD WE MET SANDY

Thank God we met Sandy

Gary Carson

Copyright
Gary Carson 2019

All rights reserved

No part of this book may be reproduced, stored in a retrieval system, or
transmitted in any form or by any means – electronic, mechanical,
photocopy, recording, or otherwise – without written permission of the
publisher, except for brief quotation in written reviews.

ISBN 978-1-913069-10-0

All Scripture References are from the King James Version (KJV)
or the New International Version (NIV). See footnotes

Front cover photograph: *Sandra viewing the city of Lisbon, Portugal,
during a Mediterranean cruise (October 2013)*

Printed by J.C. Print Limited
Email: info@jcprint.net

This book is dedicated to my son, Edward,
and his wife, Anna, who, in Sandra's own words
were her *'two precious people'*.

Proceeds from the sale of this book will
be donated to NIPanC.

*NiPanC is a Northern Ireland Pancreatic Cancer group
working in partnership with Pancreatic Cancer Action (PCA)
and Pancreatic Cancer Research Fund (PCRF)*

Foreword

"For You are with me" – A beautiful line from one of the most well-known passages in the Bible, Psalm 23. Beloved words and none more apt to describe the relationship of Gary and Sandra and their relationship with God. I first met Gary at the Pancreatic Cancer Support Group at the Mater Hospital. He had already lost Sandra and I can recall his heart-breaking story of Sandra's short journey from diagnosis to her passing. He spoke of her with warmth and love and although I never had the privilege of meeting her, I really wish I had.

As a pancreatic surgeon and having spent the last 20 years looking after patients and their families who have been affected by this most aggressive of cancers, Sandra's story of diagnosis at an advanced stage is all too common. Pancreatic cancer will soon become the second leading cause of cancer death and in the UK, approximately 10,000 people will receive this diagnosis each year. It is sometimes called the 'silent killer' with only 10% of people eligible for potentially curative surgery due to late diagnosis. Despite improvement in diagnostic tests and operative intervention, the overall survival 5-year survival has not changed in over 40 years and remains at less than 7%. Research continues into new and better treatments and charities like Pancreatic Cancer UK, Pancreatic Cancer Action and Pancreatic Cancer Research Fund work tirelessly to raise awareness of signs and symptoms and provide support to those diagnosed and their families.

Gary has written a wonderful tribute to Sandra: a story of love, faith and determination in the face of true adversity. This book will also raise awareness of pancreatic cancer and help others who are dealing with this disease, either themselves or in a loved one. Sandra's knowledge of God's love for her was never in doubt and her courage in the course of her illness, a testament to her character.

So, this is a book about faith, hope and above all, love. And whatever challenges we are facing in our lives, David's Psalm reminds us and reassures us, that we are not alone.

"And we know that in all things God works for the good of those who love Him, who have been called according to His purpose."
Romans 8 v 28 (NIV)

Mark A Taylor
Consultant Surgeon
Belfast

Preface

A simple little card came through the letterbox on what would have been Sandra's 53rd birthday. Joan, who usually sat beside her during the Sunday morning church service, had sent it. She had written, *'In loving remembrance on this your birthday. We will never forget you… till we meet again.'*

My Sandra touched the lives of so many people in a positive way. We will never forget her; I will never forget her.

I believe *'Love's last gift is remembrance'*, and so for the past few years the overwhelming desire of my broken but grateful heart, has been to tell our story; a story of blessing, grief, and yet withal, hope.

'She was truly one of a kind' – Sylvia, Sandra's Secondary School teacher. (December 2018)

'Her Gary'

Acknowledgements

During a walk one evening in January 2017, the thought of writing a book about Sandra and my subsequent journey through bereavement flashed across my mind. While the book has finally reached the printing stage I know this would not have been possible without the help of others.

Heading up this list is my good friend Alan McIlwaine, himself an author of a number of books. I am indebted to him for the countless hours spent editing and proofing the text, his sound advice on many aspects of publishing, and his writing the script for the back cover.

It has been my pleasure in recent years to meet Mark Taylor, Consultant Surgeon, and I very much appreciate his willingness to write the inspirational Foreword.

The book includes extracts from letters, texts and cards sent by so many folk whose lives were touched by Sandra. Their words vividly convey the esteem in which she was held and I offer my sincere thanks to those who sent them, with no idea where they would eventually appear.

As indicated elsewhere in this book, I am indebted to the charities named therein for the very latest information regarding pancreatic cancer. I trust that I have presented this information in a satisfactory way. If not, I apologise in advance.

Sincere thanks also to J.C. Print Ltd for managing the publishing process in such a sensitive and professional manner.

Above all, I am thankful to my Heavenly Father for his preserving grace, and for placing the initial thought in my mind to write this book.

Gary Carson

Table of Contents

'A wife of noble character who can find?
She is worth far more than rubies.' [1]

CHAPTER 1

Finding Sandra

Thursday, 3rd November 1983, began like any other day in the
Department of Finance Accounts Branch in Parliament Buildings,
Stormont, Belfast – processing invoices upon invoices! Somehow,
you never seemed to reach the bottom of the pile! However, it would
prove to be no ordinary Thursday. This day would completely change
the course of my life.

I had joined the Northern Ireland Civil Service (NICS) as a Clerical
Assistant (CA) almost 4 years earlier on Monday, 19th November
1979, after having left the protective environment of Orangefield
Boys' Secondary School in East Belfast the previous Friday. My highly
respected and inspirational English teacher, Mr Francis, had rightly
cautioned me that the position was just the first rung of a very tall
ladder. Nevertheless, I reckoned that it was a secure job in the
turbulent Northern Ireland of the late 1970s. I would also receive the
princely, and not to be scoffed at, sum of £32.13 a week! That was
too good an offer to turn down.

I am pleased to say that after working as a CA for just over a year I
reached the second rung of that ladder and was promoted to Clerical
Officer (CO). Personnel Branch notified me of my success and sent
an accompanying form upon which I was expected to indicate my
preferences regarding a new posting. That was easy – any job as long

---

[1] Proverbs 31:10 (NIV)

as it did not involve a lot of figure work! I owe a great debt of gratitude to quite a few of the Orangefield teachers who inspired me to achieve several 'O' Level grades that I never thought possible when leaving primary school. Unfortunately, Mathematics was not one of them and my *Grade 3 Certificate in Secondary Education*, for those not conversant with the educational qualifications of that era, was not something to boast about. You can imagine my dismay when I was duly sent to an Accounts Branch. After 39 years in the NICS, I am pleased to report that career development is somewhat more robust nowadays.

Anyhow, on that November morning I quietly popped out of the office for a few minutes to make a telephone call. This was a call that couldn't be made sitting in a room surrounded by colleagues, so I made my way downstairs to one of the tiny telephone kiosks located close to the front entrance of Parliament Buildings, and closed the narrow door. Ah, privacy! Remember, the world of communications was very different in those days since mobile phones, texting and the whole social media platform were almost a couple of decades away.

I quickly dialled the number of the Automobile Association Travel Agency at Fanum House on Great Victoria Street, Belfast, to speak to Miss Sandra McClean, one of its female travel consultants. The call was not to discuss any cheap holidays that might have been on offer, but rather, something of a more personal nature. Upon exchanging initial pleasantries I managed to bravely get to the point and posed what was arguably the most significant question I have ever asked, "What are you doing tonight?" Sandra promptly replied, "I'm ironing!" Undeterred, I responded by enquiring if she would be ironing all night. To my relief, the answer was 'No' and she agreed to meet me later that evening.

The rendezvous point would be outside the Tullycarnet Bowling Club, Dundonald at 9pm – hardly the most romantic spot in the world. However, I knew where it was, and I hoped that we could then go for a drive, and if things went well, a romantic walk along the coast. My mind was now racing ahead and my heart was beating much faster. I returned to the office with that extra spring in my step. Somehow, that mundane pile of invoices didn't bother me so much anymore. As I look back, I wonder how I managed to concentrate long enough to process any of them correctly that afternoon.

It had been anything but a random phone call, though, as I had known Sandra long before 3rd November 1983, having met in our early teenage years. Samuel, my best friend at school, had invited me to a Young Peoples group that met every Saturday evening in the Iron Hall on Templemore Avenue, East Belfast. He was in a steady relationship with Sandra's younger sister, Linda, and consequently, our paths often crossed, giving us the opportunity to get to know each other. All very platonic at that time I should add.

On Sunday mornings, I attended my own church, Ballyhackamore Gospel Hall, which was a couple of miles away on the Upper Newtownards Road. As I walked home with my friend Tom, I was frequently alerted by the sound of a Chrysler Avenger's horn. It was Sandra passing by with her family and she would always wave. While I sometimes wondered why she waved so enthusiastically, I never imagined that romance would ever be in the offing. Sandra had a unique, and never changing magnetism all of her own. Both male and female friends craved her company, and I knew that she had plenty of suitors.

Teenage years came and went, and my attendance at the Young People's group with it. This meant that I wasn't seeing as much of Sandra. However, I was invited to Samuel and Linda's wedding on 2nd July 1983 and observed that she had lost none of her youthful beauty and charm. Just a few months later we met each other again at evening church services in Holborn Hall, Bangor and Scrabo Hall, Newtownards. My 21st birthday party on 26th October 1983 (two days before my actual birthday) was held at the Tullycarnet Bowling Club – soon to become 'the rendezvous point' – and Sandra and I chatted, as always, but somehow we were now seeing each other in a different light. I knew that she was presently 'unattached' and seeds of attraction were beginning to take root.

Anyhow, back to 3rd November 1983. After leaving work that afternoon I attended the Neighbourhood Family Hour at my own church and afterwards drove quickly over to Tullycarnet. Sandra was waiting at the agreed spot. I never doubted for a minute that she would not be there. We then went for that romantic walk in Crawfordsburn Country Park. Conversation came naturally that dark winter's night. A warm fire, that never died, was lit in our hearts.

Sandra often laughed about our first kiss underneath my umbrella as the rain fell that night. She would also remind me that before leaving her home that night I had commented that it wasn't healthy to see each other every night because we still needed to make time for our friends, fulfil family responsibilities, and so on. Sandra, understandably, wondered if I was diplomatically telling her not to take the relationship too seriously. In fact, nothing could have been further from the truth. I soon realised that my seemingly sensible remark was much easier said than done, because we met up again that weekend! We were soon spending most evenings together and it wasn't long before we were visiting each other's homes and attending church services together on a regular basis.

As a young Christian I sought assurance that God was overseeing our relationship and was struck by the Scripture that said: *'Call unto me, and I will answer thee, and shew thee great and mighty things, which thou knowest not.'* [2] On three distinct occasions the verse came to my notice and I shared this with Sandra. Thereafter, it remained close to our hearts. It is written on the flyleaf of the Bible that Sandra gave me for my 22nd Birthday in October 1984, and indeed, on the Bible that I then gave her on her 23rd Birthday in May 1985. I also quoted it in my wedding speech the following year.

---

[2] Jeremiah 33:3 (KJV)

The bond between Sandra and me grew increasingly strong as we openly shared our hopes and dreams. We were totally relaxed in each other's company and felt as though we were destined to be together. Within three weeks of that walk through Crawfordsburn Park I told Sandra that, God willing, we would be married within three years!

The 3rd November became our 'special day' every year and took the place of Valentine's Day so to speak. On that date in 2012 I texted Sandra while sitting on the bus travelling into work in Belfast and reminded her that it was 29 years since our first date, and that I was still glad she had not been 'ironing all night'. She replied expressing her appreciation for my text, her surprise at the sudden realisation that it was as many as 29 years, and of her hope that there would be many more years to come. Alas, it was not to be.

I usually bought Sandra a gift of some description on our 'special day' each year. So, on 3rd November 2013 – our last special day together – I called at the Argento shop in Newtownards Shopping Centre to buy a charm for her ever expanding Pandora bracelet. When it came to buying gifts, I was habitually indecisive – as in so many other aspects of my life – and yet, that afternoon I instantly purchased a particular charm that seemed to stand out in a display cabinet at the counter. Just two words were inscribed: *'Forever together'*. I genuinely thought we would be.

CHAPTER 2

Living with Sandra

As 1984 dawned, our relationship continued to blossom, and as with couples in love, we spent much of our free time together. We began to talk excitedly of going on holiday with Linda and Samuel who, of course, were married the previous year. Everything was duly booked for 10th July, so off we headed via the Larne-Stranraer ferry to Scotland's Glasgow Airport to catch a flight to the serene Greek island of Rhodes for two weeks. The sun shone, and I have many pleasant memories of beautiful food, gift shops, site seeing, and for me, a break from those countless invoices. Admittedly, there was that infamous trip to the small island of Symi during which we learned that Greek boats did not cope particularly well with the rough waters along the Turkish coast. Let's say, the vessel made that Larne-Stranraer car ferry a few days earlier seem like the QE2!

Nevertheless, a much more sinister incident occurred just after the return flight from Rhodes landed in Glasgow. As we travelled through the suburbs of Paisley well into the evening, a stolen car was driven over the top of a painted roundabout directly in front of us, and hit Samuel's Vauxhall Astra Estate. The stolen car, a Vauxhall Viva, ricocheted of the Astra damaging its wing and headlight, before going on to strike the central reservation on what was a busy main road. It then proceeded to perform a series of somersaults before crashing into a Mercedes car parked at a corner pub and landing on its roof.

---

[3] The words written on a painting, given to us by my Aunt Joan as a wedding gift, which adorned our living room throughout married life.

It was a scene truly reminiscent of an episode of the US police drama of that era, *'Starsky and Hutch'*. We sat shocked and seemingly glued to our seats. I was convinced that the occupants of the Viva could not have survived, but amazingly, they did, and into the bargain, had fled the scene! An ambulance promptly arrived and after the paramedics checked that we were not injured, albeit somewhat paler, we were able to travel on to Stranraer for the ferry home – with just one headlight.

In those few crazy moments our lives were very much on the line. Had the stolen car struck the side of Samuel's car rather than the front wing, it is sobering to think that Samuel, and Sandra, who was sitting directly behind him, would have been seriously injured, if not killed. Life could subsequently have been so very different. Sandra and I may never have experienced the joy of marriage, never mind either couple having children. How thankful I am to the Lord that He preserved us from serious harm that summer's night on the outskirts of Glasgow.

As the year ended, Sandra and I attended a World Focus Missionary Conference held 27th December 1984 to 1st January 1985 in Gormanston College, County Meath. I had been to a similar event three years earlier, but how meaningful it now was attending with Sandra. We were each confronted with the challenge of living our young lives for Christ in a world that needed to hear the gospel. While we didn't return to Northern Ireland with any sense of 'a calling' to missionary work, we did return with strengthened faith and a closer relationship with each other as the new year stretched out before us.

By this time the subject of engagement was regularly featuring in our conversation, so I asked Sandra what had been her longest relationship. When she told me 18 months I duly suggested getting engaged on the 3rd June 1985 i.e. exactly 19 months since our first date at Crawfordsburn! For some reason or other that seemed appropriate to me. Needless to say, I wanted her dad's approval beforehand and so at his 60th birthday dinner on 30th April, in the old Barclay Restaurant at Shaw's Bridge, I asked Albert McClean if I could have his daughter's hand in marriage. He gladly gave his consent and Sandra promptly accepted my marriage proposal that same night.

The 3rd June duly arrived and we went excitedly to Gardiner Brothers on Waring Street, Belfast. I fondly recall the trays of rings being brought out and me pressing my leg against Sandra's under the table when I thought a particular ring was that little bit too expensive for a humble civil servant! Sandra smiled profusely though, when she chose her sapphire and diamond ring. Throughout our years together, she often reminded me that I would still need to buy her an emerald – her favourite stone – one day. While not an emerald, she did finally get another special ring in June 2011 during a holiday to Mexico to mark our 25th Wedding Anniversary. That day brought another contented smile.

I go back to the summer of 1985 and those happy, carefree days of youth, when we boldly decided to go off on holiday by ourselves to the Lake District, Morecambe and Blackpool. Lakes, amusement arcades and shopping filled those lovely summer days. We often joked about a little café in Penrith where we had stopped on Sunday afternoon for lunch – my rubber beef burger, Sandra's carrot coloured tomato soup, the sugar heaped somewhat uncouthly into a breakfast cereal bowl, and a Lucozade bottle being used for the ketchup! I dread to think what hygiene rating it would receive today. The owner commented, "Much obliged" as we paid the bill. Driving away, we laughed until we cried, before I was forced to pull the car over to the side of the road for safety reasons! It's strange how some of the little things in life linger so clearly in one's memory.

Sandra and I never envisaged a long engagement, so after returning home we began planning our wedding. It wasn't long before the date was set: 27th August 1986. But where would we go to live? We had always assumed it would be close to our families in East Belfast. However, none of the houses in that area seemed to tick the right boxes – especially with regard to price – so we concluded that maybe a house outside Belfast would be a better option.

One evening, while driving in Newtownards we spotted a charming little semi-detached bungalow in the Rosehill area. It had been built just three years earlier and required no remedial work. Considering my distinct limitations in the field of DIY, this suited me very well. I reckoned that both our fathers could help with the minor interior redecoration and garden restoration work. We promptly contacted Peter Rogers Estate Agents and the Nationwide Building Society, and on Sandra's birthday, Saturday, 17th May 1986 – just before leaving to attend the wedding of our friends Sylvia and Alan – we received confirmation that the mortgage had been approved. Consequently, the house was purchased, and it became our home for the duration of our married life.

As the 'big day' itself approached, life was characterised by busy planning: invitations, wedding cars, suits, flowers, a honeymoon and seemingly endless parties to view presents as was the custom of the day. While we would be married in the Iron Hall, Belfast, Sandra was content to leave there and join me at Ballyhackamore Gospel Hall. On her last Sunday morning attending the Iron Hall, Pastor Jack Mitchell announced that their 'dear sister, Sandra McClean' was to be married later that week and that she was going to join 'the Brethren'. He jested, "I don't know what Sandra is going to do because women have to remain silent in their meetings!"

On Wednesday, 27th August, the guests gathered for the wedding at 12 noon. My punctuality had been the source of one or two disagreements during our courtship, so on this occasion I was determined to be on time. Sandra, however, did not walk up the isle until 12.45pm! I had paced around the small room at the front of the main hall several times wondering what could have happened. The registrar from Belfast City Council declared that he was giving her 15 more minutes. Hearing that only added to my anxiety. Sandra calmly explained that the wedding cars had parked a short distance from her home and that the drivers never came to knock the door. While the photographer was in attendance, the videographer was not, and missed the entire wedding ceremony! He only arrived when the confetti was being brushed away from the front of the church. Other than that, everything else went according to plan.

My beautiful Sandra walked down the aisle with her proud dad to the strains of the bridal chorus, *Here comes the bride* from the opera *'Lohengrin'* by Richard Wagner. She wore a white dress and hat, and of course, her Magie Noire fragrance. We exchanged vows and rings, and barely thought about those words 'till death us do part' in the euphoria of the moment. Surely such words only related to a time when we would be old and grey. Pastor Mitchell gave his blessing: "I pronounce you man and wife." Two hearts were joined together in love. Two lives became one. I suspect I didn't appreciate the full significance of the marriage bond back then.

We heartily sang our favourite hymns and listened intently to Pastor Mitchell's address before leaving the church with the organist playing the very familiar *Trumpet Voluntary*. A sea of smiling faces greeted us as we ventured outside. The poor weather experienced across Northern Ireland during the previous few days – caused by the remnants of Hurricane Charley that had made its way across the Atlantic from the United States – had been replaced by glorious sunshine.

The reception was held in the Culloden Hotel outside Holywood (Northern Ireland!) and I will be forever indebted to Sandra's mum and dad for their kindness. Photographs and a video were taken, with the videographer doing his level best to capture every moment to compensate for his late arrival at the church. As was the norm in those days, speeches *followed* the meal, and our hearts were warmed by the expressions of good will. It was then a case of vacating the reception room by 6pm since there were no evening celebrations back then. Sandra, now suitably attired in her pink 'going away outfit', and I made it safely out of the hotel grounds in a car rattling with tins and plastered in foam and party string.

As we drove away, our now forgiven videographer asked if I had any particular music that he could use with the video footage. I hastily reached into the glove box and handed him a Richard Clayderman cassette (remember these?) with a number of piano recitals. What was a mistake! While he subsequently selected several appropriate pieces, he happened to include *Yesterday* by the Beatles – hardly the most suitable lyrics.

> *Yesterday all my troubles seemed so far away.*
> *Now it looks as though they're here to stay.*
> *Oh, I believe in yesterday.*[4]

His choice, nevertheless, brought smiles to our faces over the years and provided me with at least one funny story to retell when asked to make a speech at someone else's wedding. The video ended with the song, *She wears my ring,* and I was so proud that Sandra did, and with the accompanying sub title, *'Not the end – just the beginning.'* It was indeed the beginning of almost 28 precious years together.

Those who know me will not be in the least bit surprised to hear that my first destination after leaving the Culloden Hotel that evening was a garage on the Comber Road, Dundonald. I went there to remove the tin cans and wash the car! That was soon followed by a trip to Bangor to purchase a beef burger in the famous Burger County on the sea front. Charlie, the proprietor, understandably looked rather bemused when I commented that I had just got married earlier that afternoon.

Sandra had the honour of the next call as we visited Pastor Mitchell and his wife before travelling back to the Culloden for the night. The pastor lived a short distance away and Sandra simply wanted to give him her flowers so that he could in turn give them to folk during his pastoral visits. That gesture was so typical of Sandra. I vividly recall how Pastor Mitchell eventually told us to *'Go'* at 11.45pm,

---

[4] https://www.azlyrics.com/lyrics/beatles/yesterday.html

acknowledging, that while he had married many couples over the years, none had ever stayed at his home on their wedding night till almost midnight!

Leaving the hotel the following morning, we drove to the Belfast International Airport for our flight to London and then on to the Island of Crete for our honeymoon. On the way, however, I thought it best to stop at the Nationwide Building Society in Glengormley in order to pay our mortgage just in case we spent the money abroad! That turned out to be a wise decision as we did return home with empty pockets! Indeed, within a few days of arriving in Crete we had purchased a rather expensive oil painting.

The painting depicts a beach close to our resort during what appears to have been stormy conditions, and yet in the foreground a little boat rests serenely on the shore. Looking back, I recall its cost and how that we had to survive on rations, so to speak, for the final couple of days. (There were no credit cards and no 'hole in the wall' dispensing back then!) Bill and Marjorie, a lovely middle-aged English couple whom we got to know in the hotel, intuitively sensed our plight and invited us out for dinner on the final evening. Despite our protestations, they refused to take no for an answer. (Sandra warned me not to order steak!) We were very grateful though, and shortly after arriving back home Sandra characteristically sent them a lovely Irish linen tablecloth. Sandra and Marjorie went on to exchange lengthy letters each Christmas.

As indicated, we returned home to our new life together in Newtownards, and in 1989 our lives changed dramatically in the most blessed way. Sandra fell pregnant, and our precious son Edward was born on 14th September. He had not been due until early October, but the consultant thought it wise to bring the planned caesarean section forward given his concerns about Sandra's blood pressure. We had received wedding invitations for the 13th and 15th September but Sandra was more than happy to miss both – while I had the enjoyment of all three!

At around 10.30am on the morning of Edward's birth I waited for what seemed a lifetime in the family room at the Jubilee Maternity Wards of the Belfast City Hospital. A nurse eventually brought me over a little bundle of life and asked me what I had hoped for. I hesitated before indicating that I simply wanted the baby to be well. However, when she announced that we had a son, I couldn't contain my joy. Ironically, Sandra and I had sat at her bedside the night before discussing suitable names and without knowing the gender agreed that the next morning we would call 'him' Edward. He later became Eddie to almost everyone – except us.

It would be over a week before mother and baby were released from the hospital due to Edward having developed jaundice, but not before Sandra had endeared herself to the midwife, Mary Lou. In due course we were invited to Mary Lou and Mark's wedding. Sandra was truly blessed with a unique personality that enabled her to develop close friendships with persons who were once complete strangers, and here was yet another striking example.

We would have loved another child, but that was taken out of our hands with the passage of time. I can't help but smile, though, when I recall how my grandmother often asked Sandra why she wanted another child when we had a son like Edward. To this day he remains a son to be immensely proud of. Parenting was very easy for us as Edward gave us no sleepless nights – except one or two as a baby of course!

Edward had a very special relationship with his mum. She talked to him honestly and openly about every facet of his life. I fondly remember him saying on more than one occasion, "Mum I don't believe you just asked me that!" When, as a small boy, he talked about the lessons he learned at Sunday school, and of the fact that he wanted to be in Heaven, it was Sandra who prayed with him, and helped him in his childlike understanding of the gospel message, and it was her who led him to faith in the Lord Jesus. Edward grew in stature, and so did that faith.

As parents, we were thrilled when Edward graduated from the University of Ulster on 4th July 2012 with a BA in Fine and Applied Art. We were, however, even more overjoyed just a few days earlier when, on 26th June 2012, during a family holiday to Florida, he got engaged to his long-time girlfriend, Anna, at Cinderella Castle in Disneyworld. Exactly one year later to the day, they then married in Scrabo Hall, Newtownards where they were both members. It is amazing to think that this was the church Sandra and I had visited together just a few days before beginning our own relationship back in 1983.

I will be forever thankful to God that Sandra enjoyed all those happy moments before the tragic events of 2014 unfolded. During those dark days Edward and Anna remained her inspiration. The following telephone text, sent shortly after her cancer diagnosis, said it all, *'Nite nite my 2 precious people. Plz get some rest xx. Love you both so much xx. You've given me hope!! Xx'*

Throughout our married life, despite living in Newtownards, Sandra and I remained at Ballyhackamore Gospel Hall where she took an active part in so many of the church activities. Sandra not only attended services, but was also a leader in the *Every Girls Rally* (a spiritual, physical and educational organisation for young girls); a Sunday school teacher and Youth Camp leader and occasional cook as well. At the Sunday school outings and prize-giving meetings, children and their parents huddled around her seeking attention as she greeted them with that beaming smile.

When it came to the more mundane things in the church such as cleaning, Sandra also played her part. Never satisfied with just hovering and dusting, she often spent considerably longer than I thought necessary, making sure that the glass doors were gleaming! During such cleaning sessions she had the unforgettable habit of switching on the microphone and going up to the pulpit to sing. And she could sing! Invariably she chose a hymn that her dad had sung: *Does Jesus Care?* [5] How very poignant!

---

[5] Frank E. Graeff (1860–1919)

Does Jesus care when my heart is pained
Too deeply for mirth or song,
As the burdens press, and the cares distress,
And the way grows weary and long?

Refrain:
Oh, yes, He cares, I know He cares,
His heart is touched with my grief;
When the days are weary, the long nights dreary,
I know my Saviour cares.

Does Jesus care when my way is dark
With a nameless dread and fear?
As the daylight fades into deep night shades,
Does He care enough to be near?

Does Jesus care when I've tried and failed
To resist some temptation strong;
When for my deep grief there is no relief,
Though my tears flow all the night long?

Does Jesus care when I've said 'goodbye'
To the dearest on earth to me,
And my sad heart aches till it nearly breaks –
Is it aught to Him? Does He see?

I often told Sandra, as she sang, that I was going to announce her as the soloist some week. Time after time I received the same reply, "Aye, right!"

Over the years I was regularly invited to speak at other churches on Sunday evenings (mainly across counties Antrim and Down) and Sandra would faithfully accompany me. While I sought the Lord's help in presenting the gospel, I was reassured each time when I looked down from the pulpit and saw Sandra smiling back as only she could.

I am disappointed that so few people waited to speak to me afterwards regarding my message. On the other hand, I have fond memories of standing at the door shaking hands while a group of women surrounded her. We came as a package; you didn't get one without the other.

Through all the experiences of marriage – the happy days, the sad days, the days when we laughed, the days when we cried, the days when we were in total agreement, and also the days when we didn't quite see eye-to-eye – we grew to love each other more deeply. Our relationship was built upon our Christian faith. We had both given our lives to the Lord Jesus Christ as young children; me on 29th June 1977 and Sandra, while even younger, on 4th February 1969. We disappointed our Saviour on countless occasions, both individually and as a couple, yet He truly blessed our marriage. He had promised to show us 'great and mighty things', and He did.

'Sandra...from the Greek meaning "defender of men".' [6]
Be happy is her motto. Always there to help –
she is a friend to everyone. The intrigue of
foreign travel lures her.'

CHAPTER 3

Travelling with 'Sandy'

At birth, Sandra's mum, Sadie, had wanted to name her Sandra, while her dad, Albert, favoured Caroline. In the end, she got 'Sandra Caroline'. The name Sandra was certainly appropriate as the words at the top of this page illustrate. However, throughout her career in the travel industry, and indeed amongst many of her friends, she was just 'Sandy'. In recognition of this, and in some measure a tribute to her colleagues, I will simply refer to her as Sandy in the remainder of this chapter.

After leaving school in 1978, Sandy got her first taste of booking holidays while working for her lifelong friend, Arthur Carnaghan, at Arcadia Travel in the Queen's Arcade, Belfast. The company specialised in coach tours to Ireland, and Arthur often reminds me of their numerous trips down South to check out routes and hotels. Apparently, but not, surprisingly, the evenings were frequently filled with laughter and those long journeys there and back were never tedious. When leaving Arcadia Travel, Arthur's employee reference letter, dated 10th November 1981, simply stated, *'...her time keeping and honesty are beyond reproach.'*

---

[6] http://scalar.usc.edu/works/wiki/baby-names/sandra-name-meaning

That first job unquestionably gave Sandy a real desire to work in the Travel business. So, on 10th December 1981, following a successful interview, she was offered a position in the Automobile Association (AA) Travel Agency at Fanum House on Great Victoria Street, Belfast, which she took up on 4th January 1982. There, she developed her knowledge of worldwide travel and proudly attained her *Certificate of Travel Agency Competence (COTAC)*. Sandy remained with the AA until 6th April 1990 when the company decided to end its package holiday business across the UK axing some 500 jobs in the process. From a personal perspective, though, the redundancy was perfect timing since Edward had been born the previous September and we agreed that it was probably best if she were to take further time off following maternity leave.

The economic climate in the early 1990s was, to say the least, somewhat challenging. Many will remember the UK recession when interest rates rose to the dizzy heights of 15% at one point. Life was tough for a newly married couple as monthly mortgage payments soared, so Sandy's life as a 'housewife' was rather short-lived. Consequently, she applied for part-time work, and as it happened, returned to the AA as a temporary retail sales assistant for a few months during 1991.

Sadly though, we had much more than finance to worry about that year as Sandra's beloved dad was diagnosed with bowel cancer. Despite initial hopes that surgery had been successful, Albert passed away just two years later on 29th May 1993 after his own brave battle with this awful disease, but not before Sandy had made him proud of her achievements at work.

Sandy's bubbly personality always shone through and was viewed as a major asset by employers. A case in point was the fact that, having finally left the AA, she attended interviews with the Berkshire nylon factory (Newtownards), the Old Mill Coffee Shop (Dundonald) and the Belfast Telegraph during September 1991, and was offered employment by all three!

After some deliberation, Sandy accepted the sales job with the Belfast Telegraph, which involved knocking on doors across the Ards and North Down areas in an attempt to get folk signed up for the Home Delivery service. Customers, who did so, received a free set of kitchen knives which proved to be a significant incentive in some places. Nevertheless, I think Sandy's euphoric sales pitch had a greater impact than those knives! This commission based work was only for a few hours two or three nights per week and proved relatively lucrative, if not, convenient. At least, that was until one rather unproductive winter's night when she returned home very wet and cold – sapping to be more precise – and declared, "That's it, I've had enough of that!" I really couldn't blame her and that ended her days with the 'Tele'.

The truth is, Sandy's heart lay in Travel, and once Edward was a little older she returned to what she did best – selling holidays. During those early 1990s she went on to work at –

- Knock Travel, Belfast (January to August 1993)
- Laser Travel, Newtownards (January to September 1994)
- C-More Travel, Newtownards (September 1994 to August 1995)

Sandy's next job, though, was to be the most significant of her career when she took up a sales consultant position with the global travel agency, Thomas Cook. The employment began on a part-time basis at the Bloomfield Shopping Centre, Bangor on 28th Aug 1995, and she remained with the company for almost 17 years. Most of that time was spent in the Donegal Place and Donegal Square branches in Belfast city centre where she held a variety of positions that reflected the esteem with which she was held. These included –

- World Travel Specialist
- Cruise Co-ordinator for her branch, and later for the region
- Wedding and Honeymoon Co-ordinator
- Ski and Sport Co-ordinator

Needless to say, there were a number of perks in Travel. Those in the trade generally referred to them as 'educational trips'. Sandy experienced life on board some of the world's leading cruise ships such as those operated by Silversea, Seabourn and Cunard, and visited some of the most beautiful countries in the world. I think of how she tried her best to enlighten me on the differences between a typical cruise ship and an ocean liner!

I smile when I recall an invitation for both of us to attend the wedding of one of her colleagues, with the reception to be held in the Stormont Hotel, Belfast. Having already accepted the invite, Sandy was asked if she would be interested in participating in a one-week trip to Barbados – business class, at that. It wasn't difficult to choose between the wedding and the easternmost island in the Caribbean. Sandy assured me that I knew most of her work colleagues, and that I would be fine taking plenty of photographs. So, off Sandra went to visit the appropriately named 'Sandy Lane' to experience life on this paradise island. Looking back, it is strange when I recall how she told me, "Sure you still go; you know Trevor and can sit with him." Indeed, I did spend the day with her close friend Trevor, who would also tragically die of cancer just a few months ahead of Sandy.

As I browsed through Sandy's work folders I came across a rather tongue-in-cheek 'letter to prove identity' from John, one of her Thomas Cook managers, when she was asked to participate in a trip to France organised by the Paris Travel Service. It simply stated: *This letter is to certify that "OH MY NERVES" is going to Paris on 7 April 1997. She is currently employed by Cook's in Bangor and this trip is in connection with work related business. Should you need clarification give us a ring.'* That renowned expression was synonymous with Sandy and fondly adopted by many of her colleagues over the years.

Yes, these were rightly described as 'perks of the trade'. However, in reality they were tiring trips and certainly not complimentary holidays since travel consultants were often whisked from hotel to hotel to attend lectures and presentations. No one should be under any illusion as to the pressures that go with the job. Customers expect every facet of a holiday to go smoothly and are quick to complain if even the smallest mistake is made. A holiday abroad can be the highlight of the year and woe betide anyone who messes it up! Checking and double checking flight schedules and arranging around the world holidays, weddings and honeymoons in some of the world's remotest resorts, was often far from straightforward. Sandy routinely went that extra mile to make sure there were no hitches. More than that, she sometimes even gave customers her personal mobile number as a precaution should they encounter problems.

As with all retail business, income targets were the name of the game and Sandy, like the rest of her colleagues, was expected to achieve these on a consistent basis. I am filled with pride when I peruse the Thomas Cook certificates congratulating her on her successes when, for example, she was 'Top Seller' during January 2007 and April 2007 with individual sales of £122,144 and £53,117 respectively – no mean feat any month, especially back then. Such certificates reflected her professional competence and dedication to the company.

Considerable patience is required in the Travel business. Without naming customers Sandy occasionally told me of those who were unsure of where they wanted to go, and indeed, of how their budgets often didn't match rather lofty expectations in terms of the resort or the standard of accommodation. Despite having to meet the stretching targets, Sandy was never happy taking that all-important deposit if a customer showed the slightest bit of hesitancy. She needed to see that spark of excitement in their eyes. Customers seemed to appreciate the absence of high-pressure sales and invariably returned after reviewing the options Sandy had given them, to make a booking.

When Thomas Cook took the decision to close its High Street branches in early 2012 Sandy wondered if her career in Travel was drawing to an end. She needed not have worried though, because the phone rang at home on Saturday, 25th February 2012 with the caller asking to speak to Sandy Carson. It was Delia Aston from Clubworld Travel to ask if she would be interested in going to work in their new branch in East Belfast. Sandy welcomed the prospect of a fresh challenge and took the opportunity to also mention Susan, her close friend in Thomas Cook, who, too, was being made redundant. Sandy was delighted when they were both selected following interviews on Friday, 9th March 2012. So, as the Thomas Cook door closed on 3rd May 2012, a new door into Clubworld opened just a few days later on 8th May 2012.

Sandy's time in Clubworld may have been brief, but in just over two years she established new friendships and new customers. Later in this book I will comment upon the esteem with which Delia and her husband, Stephen, held her. For the moment, though, I reflect on some of the conversations I overheard Sandy having with Delia as we drove home together in the evenings. One could have been forgiven for thinking that Sandy was a partner in the business rather than an employee!

One of the blessings that came from marrying a travel consultant was the benefit of discounted holidays. We both loved going on holiday and Sandy frequently brought home lovely glossy brochures showcasing some of the world's most beautiful resorts. When it came to deciding how to spend any savings accrued during the year, the option of a holiday generally took precedence over other considerations such as home improvements, a second car, etc. Wonderful memories come flooding back of golden beaches in Greece and Spain, the romantic city of Paris, the amazing jungles of Mexico, the picturesque blue mountains of Jamaica, the neon lights of Times Square in New York and the stately grandeur of George Square in Glasgow where we celebrated our 25th Wedding Anniversary. However, I reckon we would never seriously have exchanged any of them for the simplicity of Conway Square in Newtownards!

Of course, the whole family benefited from Sandy's job, and August 2000 stands out as a group of 19 travelled by Flexibus to Belfast International Airport en route to Salou in Spain. Sandy delighted in co-ordinating this unique family vacation. To be honest, we were never content unless we were taking one, or sometimes, two, of Linda's children with us, and our son Edward was ever grateful for his cousins' company. John, Anne-Louise, Emma and Naomi (who at times can bear an uncanny resemblance to her Auntie Sandy), were more like his brother and sisters than his cousins. It was a delight in later years when Anna also joined us on those happy summer trips abroad.

At the end of June 2003 we had the privilege of visiting Orlando in Florida. We had travelled by bus (that's another story) to Disneyland, Paris for a couple of days back in July 1997 when we, metaphorically speaking, caught the 'Disney bug'. That first holiday in the USA captivated us. We were probably a bit too sentimental, but the truth is, we shed tears reading the words on the plaque at the entrance to the Magic Kingdom – *'May Walt Disney World bring joy and inspiration and new knowledge to all who come to this happy place… a Magic Kingdom where the young at heart of all ages can laugh and play and learn together.'* [7] I'm thankful that we experienced that joy and inspiration during six further visits when we laughed, played and learned together as a family. These are priceless memories.

While Sandy had travelled on several of those amazing cruise ships, my experience of sea travel had essentially been limited to the 'roll-on, roll-off' car ferries to Scotland. It is, therefore, moving to recall that our very last holiday together, in September 2013, was a cruise to the Mediterranean with our friends Mervyn and Pamela. Going to bed in one country, and waking up next morning in a different country, was an altogether new experience. I began to appreciate why 'mature couples', perhaps tiring of beach holidays, opt to go on a cruise. This was much more sedate compared to the hustle, bustle and excitement of Florida. As the ship left Southampton Port on a

---

[7] http://www.azquotes.com/author/44266-Roy_O_Disney

tranquil Sunday evening, I turned to Mervyn and said, "This is as good as it gets." How true those words would prove to be. In January 2014 we booked another cruise for September of that year, but going on it was not to be.

I could not possibly write about Sandy's occupation without including comments from her loyal customers. What did they think of Sandy, and of the service she had provided? The following letters and feedback forms provide a remarkable and heart-warming insight into 'travelling with Sandy' –

The reason I am writing is that for the past six years we have booked our holidays with XXXX and have never had the standard of service that we received from Sandy who quite happily spent approximately one hour with us, searching and explaining everything, until we were quite happy with our choice – other agents we had visited merely check one operator or resort and when this proved unsuitable were happy to let us go and move on to the next customer. In these times when people are quick to complain about poor service it is important that we recognise the good and I can honestly say that Sandy is a credit to your company and deserves to be congratulated on her customer service standards. I can definitely say that next year Thomas Cook will be our first choice when it comes to booking a holiday. – A letter addressed to the manager in Thomas Cook in Bangor's Bloomfield Shopping Centre and signed by Mrs Hamilton (October 1998)

I am writing this in the hope that you can pass on my praise and thanks to one of your members of staff. Myself and my husband and two children were in your branch on Monday 26 of July to book next summer's holiday in Turkey, we knew the place we wanted to go to i.e. Marmaris, but that was it. The consultant that dealt with us was called Sandy Carson and we advised her that we had not been abroad before and that we needed her help and advice. She was so helpful and really did her best to find us a suitable destination, which we feel will be a great benefit to us. Also I would like to thank her for her patience as I had won £750 of Thomas Cook vouchers at work and she did not get at all flustered by the fact that these were in £5 denominations and the fact that she had to put them in numerically in the computer...I really feel that praise is well due to Sandy. A few days later we were going through our travel documents and were not sure how the final amount was worked out - a phone call to Sandy yet again cleared this up and she was so friendly and reassuring that I felt I had to let you know this and perhaps you could pass on our thanks to Sandy – she is a great advert for Thomas Cook and I will certainly be recommending you to my family and friends. – A letter addressed to the local Thomas Cook manager and signed by Mary Monaghan (August 1999)

I called into your office on 22 July 1999 at 12.00 Noon and Sandy Carson was the Sales Consultant who helped me try to get a holiday for my family for next July. We have three children and because of this getting a holiday proved to be very difficult. I was also working with a budget. Sandy sat with me from 12.00-3.30pm! She had no lunch and tried everywhere. Eventually I booked a holiday in Ibiza. At all times Sandy was patient and pleasant. – A customer feedback form signed by M Carnaghan (July 1999)

Your Sales consultant, Sandy Carson, was most helpful in achieving for me suitable connecting air travel Belfast / Heathrow / Geneva and despite the lateness in the day remained cheerful. She is an asset to your company and your Donegal Place Belfast Branch in particular. – A customer feedback form signed by Jim McClean (March 2000)

I would like to commend one of your employees, a Mrs Sandy Carson who more than went out of her way to help us book our honeymoon for June 2001. We knew exactly where and when we wanted to go and Mrs Carson did everything she could to get us the best possible deal...as a result of the service we received we would definitely return to book future holidays with yourselves via Mrs Carson... – A customer feedback form signed by Stephen White (May 2000)

I was extremely pleased with the service I received from Thomas Cook. The Sales Consultant that dealt with me was Sandy Carson. I wish to say I found her very pleasant and of great help in booking my holiday. I think that she is a fantastic Sales Consultant and very valuable to the Belfast Branch. – An undated customer feedback form signed by Nick McCaffrey.

My wife and I booked a flight to Kenya…I wish to compliment Sandy Carson on the manner in which she made the arrangements. Usually, at the end of a good holiday there is a "well good' feeling. We have the holiday ahead of us and we already have the 'well good' feeling – due entirely to the manner and approach of Mrs Carson. Please pass on our thanks. – A quotation from holidaymakers, Mr & Mrs Campbell, in a Thomas Cook 'Customer Service Star of the Week' commendation, dated April 2001 and signed by Managing Director, Manny Fontenia-Novoa.

Of all the letters and cards, however, there is one that stands out. More than that, it was the letter which gave me the inspiration to write this book. We shall come to the contents shortly, but some may remember the infamous ash cloud incident back in April 2010. For a period of time all flights in and out of the UK, and several other European countries, were suspended due to ash from a volcanic eruption in Iceland spreading south. It brought travel chaos, especially for those who had made their own travel arrangements over the Internet, and who, consequently, were not supported by a travel agency. Sandy had gone the extra mile to help a pair of stranded Swedish schoolteachers and their children. Later that year, she received the following letter –

Sollentuna, December 2010

Dear Sandy,

Do you remember two separate Swedish teachers seated at your desk, asking for help to get home with 22 students, during the volcanic ash episode? Sandy, we remember you! Sometimes, we look at each other, shake our heads and laugh, and then we'll say, 'thank **God we met Sandy!'**

The trip home was incredible. We had a nice ferry trip from Belfast to Scotland, and the best fish 'n' chips of our lives in Stranraer! The train ride into Glasgow presented us with beautiful views of little lambs running around in the sunset, before we took the sleeper train to London. Our school had fixed a bus from there to Lille in France, through the tunnel. We spent a whole day in Lille, and at four a.m. the next morning another bus picked us up and took us through Belgium, the Netherlands, Germany, Denmark and southern Sweden, before arriving in Stockholm at six in the morning, four days late. What an adventure.

Of course, if it wasn't for you, we wouldn't have got to London, and then goodness knows when we would have come home. Thank you again – for your professional help, but also, and especially, for going out of your way to help us!

We were meaning to send you something before summer, but this won't even reach you in time for Christmas … Even though Sweden may not be quite as peaceful as it looks in these pictures, we hope it can be something for you to rest your eyes on now and then throughout the coming year.

Best wishes for the New Year!

Jenny Green and Karin Bodin,
Rudbeck Secondary School, Sollentuna, Sweden

It may sound cheesy, but it strikes me that the life which Sandy and I shared together, as husband and wife, for almost 28 years had many of the characteristics of a great holiday. We enjoyed such clear blue skies, the warmth of the sun, and only occasional showers.

'Do not boast about tomorrow,
for you do not know what a day may bring.' [8]

CHAPTER 4

Things Seen and Unseen

Sandra frequently reminded me of her dad's daily prayer regarding 'things seen and unseen'. Nothing, however, could have prepared us for the unseen events of 2014.

The year commenced like any other by celebrating New Year's Eve with our friends Heather and Trevor as we had done throughout most of our married life. Heather had been a close friend of Sandra's long before I ever came on the scene. "Happy New Year Darling!" I exclaimed; little knowing that it would be the last time I would utter those familiar words that I had spoken for over 30 years. How much we take for granted.

That last day of December 2013 stands out, but so also the last day of January 2014. Following their wedding, Edward and Anna had kindly given us a voucher for afternoon tea at the Culloden Hotel. It was due to expire that day. Sandra and I sat together at the hotel's open fire enjoying sandwiches and pastries, and a very welcome break from work. Thoughts inevitably turned to the summer and holidays.

We had such beautiful memories of that 2013 Mediterranean cruise, so we began browsing other cruise destinations on Sandra's mobile phone. "What about Alaska?" I asked. It had been our dream to go

---

[8] Proverbs 27:1 (NIV)

there ever since the 1990s when Sandra had brought home a Royal Caribbean video showing its picturesque landscape. We hoped that some day we could go; perhaps, when there were a few less bills to pay. Within a couple of minutes that Friday afternoon, Sandra telephoned her shop and the Alaskan cruise was duly booked. We would fly to San Francisco on 1st September 2014 and head off to the beautiful US state through the Golden Gate Bridge. Amazing; our dream would be fulfilled!

The excitement was palpable as we quickly drove to Edward and Anna's home in Donaghadee to give them the good news. We felt like newlyweds again contemplating our honeymoon! After Edward was born, all our holidays abroad had been with family or friends, and often both, and oh, how we had enjoyed them together. On this occasion, though, there would be just the two of us; the first time since 1988, when we had visited Greece. Sadly, we would never make it to Alaska. Sandra was going to a more beautiful place, but without me.

On Saturday, 5th April 2014, Sandra travelled to Portugal, courtesy of Clubworld Travel, to check out a number of hotels in the Algarve. It was a treasured experience; she was grateful to Delia, the Clubworld director, for sending her. (Her phone has many photographs of the food lavished upon her and the other travel consultants in her party.) Sandra texted to say, 'This is the life so much!!! Can't wait till Sept DV.' (We both routinely added those letters 'DV' – meaning, God willing – when making plans. I doubt if I stopped that day to really consider their significance.)

After Sandra had come home from Portugal, we contemplated buying a new house. We had lived in the same little semi-detached bungalow throughout our married life and occasionally spoke of moving elsewhere in Newtownards. Somehow, we never took the notion too seriously; at least, not until houses were built in the fields just a few hundred yards away at Tullynagardy. There was much soul searching after visiting the beautiful show houses. However, we eventually decided to be content with our lot, refurbish our existing home and in particular, replace the 20 year old kitchen. After all, there were still several other places to visit after Alaska.

So, after a lovely day out with Mervyn and Pamela in Carlingford on Easter Monday, a new suite was promptly ordered the following day. (Edward routinely joked that the old suite had given him a sore back!) This was followed by a visit to a kitchen showroom in Hilltown on the Wednesday, although in the end we opted to refurbish the existing one. It would be great, we thought, to have this work completed before heading off on our cruise in the autumn.

The pages of the calendar turned to May and the house makeover was in full swing. The walls downstairs were stripped, and the kitchen tiles removed. The existing oak cupboards would be sprayed cream, and the old MDF worktops given a 'granite transformation'. It is very sobering to recall how the kitchen sales rep, who arrived on Saturday, 24th May to take the worktop measurements, related how he had been with a customer who was terminally ill with cancer and how she was undecided as regards to going ahead with her order. At the time, Sandra and I both commented on such a sad story, not knowing that we would find ourselves in exactly the same position a mere two months later.

The garden shed, earmarked for the skip, would be replaced by a more substantial log cabin that would give me a bit of headroom to walk around in. While this was primarily for my pleasure, Sandra also saw it as an ideal location for the washing machine which, in turn, would enable her to finally have a dishwasher in the kitchen. Not surprisingly, she had already discussed the installation plans with our neighbour and resident plumber, Billy.

In next to no time the house was in a state of disarray, and even the small conservatory was crammed full with all the bits and pieces that were taken from the shed. It seemed stressful at the time, and yet, in hindsight, it was simply nothing compared to the storm that was about to break. How foolish it can be to 'sweat the small stuff'.

Our day jobs were also much busier than usual. Each night, walking up to the front door around 7pm, we often joked that the neighbours would likely be asking why we even bothered to come home at all. While Sandra would occasionally rebuke me for not collecting her until after 6pm, she always seemed to find something else to do as soon as I arrived at her shop. Everything had to be sorted with customer details suitably noted and filed. My having to wait for her gave me the opportunity to peruse those enticing holiday brochures though, and dream a little more.

There was, nevertheless, still time for enjoyable evenings together, and I fondly recall how we walked through the Stormont Estate to watch the Giro Italia cycle race on Friday, 9th May. I can still hear Sandra say, "Here they come!" before we stood together beside Carson's statue to get the best photographs possible. Ironically, our relationship had commenced with my call from a phone booth in the Parliament Buildings directly behind us some 30 years earlier. But now, here we were at Stormont, almost at the end of our time together, although we didn't realise it that warm balmy evening.

A week later, 17th May, was Sandra's birthday, so we spent the evening watching the FA Cup Final! This was not as inconsiderate as it no doubt appears. I had watched this annual football showpiece with my friend Desi for decades, and had invited him over on that occasion, too, before suddenly realising that the game coincided with Sandra's birthday. Not to worry I thought; he could bring his wife, Anne, and we could all enjoy our customary Saturday night Chinese takeaway. I'm glad the four of us spent that evening together, considering that we had been such good friends since our early 20's. Quite poignantly, our first holiday together as a couple – setting aside our honeymoon – was to Scotland with Desi and Anne back in August 1987.

The following day, Sandra went directly from the morning church service at Ballyhackamore to the cruise ship, *Celebrity Infinity*, docked at Belfast Port, for the purposes of seeing its facilities first hand.

However, she still arrived home in time to accompany me on a preaching engagement at Bethesda Gospel Hall, Bangor that evening. The night was rounded off with supper at another couple's house. Sandra had agreed to call with Lewis and Dorothy to explain a few things about cruising, as they had recently booked their first cruise with her. It was just another typically busy Sunday.

Sadly, May was also marked by bereavement. On Thursday, 8th May, Sandra attended the funeral of her long-time colleague and former World Travel Specialist at Thomas Cook's Donegal Square branch, Trevor McIlwaine. He had worked with Sandra during most of her time with the company, and I had often given him a lift home when collecting her in the evenings. Indeed, I had spent the day with him at that wedding several years earlier when Sandra was away enjoying her trip to Barbados.

Trevor was medically retired during his own battle with cancer. Sandra had taken him to many of his chemotherapy appointments at the City Hospital. Memorably, the evening before we set off on our Mediterranean cruise back in September 2013, and with everything packed, Sandra unexpectedly announced, "I need to visit Trevor before we go." We spent a lovely hour together chatting about the 'good old days'. How peculiar that Trevor's funeral was to be the last that Sandra attended.

Shortly after returning from the Portugal trip in April, Sandra began to complain of a sore back, and on several occasions mentioned that the chairs in the church were becoming difficult to sit on. There was nothing particularly unusual about this, though, as I remembered Sandra complaining many years earlier that her mum and dad's caravan seats were uncomfortable. This was something similar, I thought, but it wasn't. More worryingly, Sandra was sick a number of times after eating her evening meal. She told me of pains in her upper abdomen, but again, we tended to look on the bright side – at least I did. I suggested that the rich food she had eaten in Portugal – and continued to eat when attending work related promotional events in hotels across Belfast – may have been part of the problem.

Nonetheless, we decided that it was best to go to the doctor and explain the symptoms in order to put our minds at ease. We assumed there was probably a tablet that would do the trick, or maybe something that Sandra should avoid eating. Consequently, Sandra made an appointment to see a doctor on 30th May which was quickly followed by another on 5th June, notwithstanding the fact that the doctors didn't seem overly concerned. They suggested it could well be gallstones, helicobacter pylori infection in her stomach, or some other relatively minor ailment.

However, blood samples revealed elevated 'C-reactive protein' (CRP), indicating inflammation in the body. This can signal many different conditions, including cancer, cardiovascular disease, infection, and autoimmune conditions such as rheumatoid arthritis, lupus, and inflammatory bowel disease. For the first time I felt anxious as Sandra left a message on my phone to say, *'Bloods not good Love.'* Further tests would be necessary, and an appointment was made for an ultra scan at the Downe Hospital, Downpatrick on 1st July. This seemed such a long time to wait, but Sandra's symptoms apparently did not merit a 'red flag'.

The 10th June saw us attend our last wedding together. It was the marriage of Heather and Trevor's daughter, Rachel, to Matt in Monkstown Baptist Church, with the reception being held at Belfast Castle. Despite the Castle's idyllic setting and beautiful gardens, I recall how Sandra sat rather quietly inside. I remember, too, how I laughed at the traditional humorous speeches, little realizing that I wouldn't laugh out loud again for almost three years. As that day drew to a close, we stood on the balcony, gazing over Belfast Lough, contemplating a busy summer that would culminate in our cruise. Our dreams were fragile, though. As we approached Newtownards on the way home Sandra suddenly directed me to pull the car over, as she was going to be sick. My Sandra was ill, and deep down I think we both knew it, even if the doctors didn't.

The following Sunday was Father's Day and Sandra accompanied me to the morning and evening church services at Ballyhackamore. This was the last time she would do so. Despite feeling unwell, she managed to go to Roselawn Cemetery in the afternoon to visit her dad's grave, as was our custom on this particular day, and then later that evening to my cousin's house in Bangor to deliver a baby present that Sandra had purchased for his daughter's child a few weeks earlier.

The following Friday was 20th June and we were due to attend an Italian missionary evening, with a 'Taste of Italy' food experience, at Scrabo Hall. While Sandra had managed to struggle through another week at work, there was no way she was going to be able to make it to that event, and yet she encouraged me to go with the friends who had invited us. I did so, and they duly asked why Sandra was not with me. We were always together on such occasions. I explained that she was unwell and the look on my face likely said it all. I felt miserable and just wanted home as soon as possible that night.

With the 26th June came Edward and Anna's first Wedding Anniversary. How different things had been exactly two years earlier when we celebrated their engagement with them in Florida, and of course, their wedding just one year later. Life now seemed so unpredictable; we were filled with apprehension.

I spoke at Ballyhackamore's evening service on Sunday, 29th June. I had agreed to do so given the significance of the date – the 37th anniversary of the day I had decided as a young boy of 14 to accept the Lord Jesus Christ as my personal Saviour. I felt so very uncomfortable speaking without Sandra being present, and again, I simply wanted home.

Tuesday, 1st July 2014, finally came, and with it the ultra scan appointment. It was the first and only time we had visited Downe Hospital. We sat in the waiting area chatting with a friend who, coincidently, also had an appointment that afternoon. Sandra's name was called and she left us for around 20 minutes. When she returned she sounded quite upbeat. However, as we walked along the corridors Sandra explained that something had been identified on her liver. The radiographer happened to pass by at that exact moment and her facial expression worried me. The very vivid walk to the car park was a short one, but seemed to last forever.

Travelling back home to Newtownards, we scarcely knew what to say to each other. I just wanted to reassure Sandra that everything would be OK, as it usually had been after any other hospital appointment, but I couldn't. We stopped at a little coffee shop in Balloo, and probably for the first time, I realised that this could be very serious. We wouldn't have to wait long for results, though, as Sandra was to attend her doctor again just two days later.

On Thursday, 3rd July, I took Sandra into Belfast city centre to attend a meeting and arranged to pick her up again on the Lisburn Road just before lunchtime. When I arrived at the agreed rendezvous point, I noticed that she was carrying a large shopping bag. Despite struggling a little with her breathing at this stage, she had walked a considerable distance after the meeting to buy me new shirts and trousers.

Looking back, I'm convinced Sandra knew that this was a task she was unlikely to repeat for a long time. That act of kindness typified Sandra; her care for me took precedence, whatever the cost to herself. Approaching Newtownards on the way home, we stopped at the Old Mill coffee shop to have a bite to eat before the appointment with the doctor. Sandra tried to eat, but it was plain to see that she had little appetite and only did so to please me.

The next stop was Newtownards Health Centre. I recalled a number of previous occasions when I had sat there in the waiting area, but this one was entirely different. What exactly had the scans revealed? What would the implications be? Then the announcement: 'Mrs Carson.' My heart began to beat faster. Oh, the trepidation as we walked in together. The doctor explained the results, and I eagerly read the information on the computer screen in front of me. Sandra's pancreas, spleen and kidneys were 'not remarkable', although there were lesions on her liver. A further camera examination would be required to ascertain the reasons for the discomfort she was still experiencing.

The sense of relief was indescribable. I blurted out that I had been searching the NHS website every day; reading about a range of cancers and their symptoms, but the doctor calmly told me that I shouldn't be worrying unnecessarily. Sandra mentioned that we were due to go to Alaska on 1st September – only a matter of weeks away then – and asked if we should cancel the holiday. We were advised that there was no need to do so just yet. Sandra was so thankful; she had been determined to go on that holiday whatever the cause of her illness.

I suddenly felt 'normal' again. We crossed the road to our car and sat there for a few minutes during which time I took the opportunity to share a Bible verse with Sandra or, to be more precise, just four words within that verse. I had read it the previous weekend during my daily devotional reading – *'I will restore health.'* [9] It had given me hope, and now it could give Sandra hope, too.

Some months later, while looking through the *Notes* app on Sandra's mobile phone, I came across the following comment relative to those four words: *'Gary got this on 28th June 2014.'* I sometimes struggle to come to terms with this, but oh, the danger of taking a verse out of context to apply it to one's personal circumstances. The truth of this was to be experienced again within weeks.

We went home, and Sandra lay down after the most stressful doctor's appointment imaginable. I had a new spring in my step though, and felt reassured by the doctor's words. The heavy weight had been lifted from my shoulders. I could go upstairs with a much clearer head now and prepare a message for another meeting the following Sunday

[9] Jeremiah 30:17 (KJV)

evening at Downshire Road Hall, Holywood. Unfortunately, that tremendous sense of relief was short lived; Sandra was sick once again. Reality dawned. Sandra was still ill. Nothing had actually changed.

On Sunday, 6th July, we went to Edward and Anna's house for dinner with Sandra's mum, Sadie, and stepdad, Sammy. They later took Sandra home while I fulfilled the speaking engagement at Holywood. I had taken hundreds of Sunday services since my mid teens, but didn't realize that this would be the last time I would speak at such a meeting for well over three years. I recall another unsettling moment when the meeting was over. Noel, one of the church elders there, asked if I would give him a lift home since he had something he wished to show me. It transpired that he had a copy manuscript of the great hymn, and personal favourite of mine, *Abide with Me*, written by Henry Francis Lyte – [10]

Abide with me, fast falls the eventide:
The darkness deepens, Lord, with me abide:
When other helpers' fail, and comforts flee,
Help of the helpless, O abide with me.

Back in the 1980s Noel and I had led youth camps together in the Royal Portora School, Enniskillen, and now in his home, he reminded me of the plaque on the wall in honour of the hymn's author who had attended that school. Incidentally, I had made a point of visiting Lyte's grave in Nice during the Mediterranean cruise the previous October. Leaving Holywood that summer's evening, I wondered why this hymn had been brought to my attention in this way. Was the Lord preparing me for what lay ahead?

Another working week dawned; and Sandra was now using every last ounce of energy. Her commitment to work, her employer and her customers, was remarkable. By that stage, though, her sleeping pattern was disturbed on an almost nightly basis. The pain grew

---

[10] Henry Francis Lyte (1793–1847)

worse when she was lying down. I would often waken to find the bed empty and Sandra in the living room quietly reading her Bible. "Go back to bed Love – I'll be back in shortly" she whispered.

Thursday, 10th July, was, however, to be her last day at work. Sandra was truly exhausted. As we pulled down the shop shutter that evening, I simply said, "No more Love." I could see the pain etched across her face and it was evident that she would no longer be able to do what she had spent a lifetime doing – making people feel excited about going on holiday, wherever the destination.

When I arrived home from work the following evening, I discovered that Sandra had spent the afternoon tidying her bedroom wardrobe. It was again as if she knew something was seriously wrong and she wanted everything just right. She told me that she had been sick and it wasn't long before I witnessed her vomiting again. I simply couldn't stand by any longer and see her in this extreme discomfort. "I'm taking you to the Ulster Hospital A&E," I declared, "We have to get to the bottom of this now and can't wait for any more appointments."

Given the date, the A&E was, as anticipated, particularly busy. Some patients had been injured and others had clearly suffered as a result of alcohol abuse. Sandra was not their immediate concern. However, a doctor eventually did see Sandra and told us the results of the 9th July blood test. While the 'C-reactive protein' (CRP) reading had increased further he was not overly concerned and suggested that Sandra could have severe gastritis. There was apparently nothing more that could be done that night and she was discharged. Our minds were again briefly put at ease. The medical experts were not perturbed. Therefore, in trying to analyze the situation logically, I concluded that we, too, did not need to panic.

Traditionally, every 12th July, I would have taken my father to the Lisburn Road to watch the Parade, but not this time. Sandra often went, too, but in more recent times preferred a trip to the seaside with her friend Evelyn and her two daughters. On this occasion they had planned to go down south to Balbriggan to visit their mutual friend, Audrey, but had cancelled the trip earlier in the week knowing it was just too much for Sandra. I asked Sandra if she would like to watch the shorter Newtownards Parade in the late afternoon as I thought it would get her out of the house for an hour or so. She agreed, but again, I suspect it was for the purpose of pleasing me. That evening, we visited her mum, and from somewhere, she got the strength to dust her mum's living room; one further act of kindness and the very last time she would help in this way.

The bank holiday period commenced, and Sandra spent the week at home waiting for news of the planned gastroscopy. However, as each day passed, Sandra's strength was waning. Therefore, another doctor's appointment was made for Friday, 18th July. Further assurance was given at that consultation that the illness was probably nothing sinister, and that the camera examination should, hopefully, be arranged before the end of August. A medical certificate was issued for three weeks. There seemed nothing more that we could do. We would, somehow, have to be patient.

I left Sandra home, and prior to taking the certificate to her work, attended the funeral of a lovely Christian lady from Dundonald Gospel Hall. Dorothy had been a great encouragement with her kind reassuring words each time I had preached in her church. She had borne her own pancreatic cancer diagnosis with such grace, right to the end of her life earlier that week. As I sat with Edward at the service, I tried to imagine what it might be like to attend such a service for Sandra, but it was much too difficult a thought to process. I dismissed it from my mind.

Later that evening I asked Sandra if she would like to go out for a drive. Rather reluctantly, she agreed. We went to Millisle and gingerly walked a short distance along the beach. I thought back to some 20 years earlier when we had walked along the beach a few miles further up the coast with her dad just prior to his death from cancer. It seemed so surreal. Was history going to repeat itself? Again, I swiftly discarded those unbearable thoughts. But, as we approached the car, Sandra was sick once again. We rested for several minutes on seating overlooking the sea and ate ice cream together. We had often shared ice cream, particularly as a treat on Saturday evenings, but this would be the last time we would enjoy such a moment.

The following day, Saturday, 19th July, Sandra was particularly subdued and struggled to eat anything of substance. She complimented me on the poached eggs that I made her for lunch, but really, she couldn't face food. "Pop corn… I could try pop corn," she said, so I went and purchased a few bags in the nearby Spar. We sat quietly and watched TV together, but the film, *'Sleeping in Seattle'*, with its tale of a widower befriending another woman after the loss of his wife, brought tears to my eyes and I sensed, too, what Sandra was likely thinking. However, I purposefully continued to banish all disturbing thoughts from my mind.

'Why, you do not even know what will
happen tomorrow.
What is your life? You are a mist that appears
for a little while and then vanishes.' [11]

CHAPTER 5

The Unthinkable

20th July 2014 will be forever etched on my mind. While Sandra's skin always looked healthy, even in the few months when she hadn't felt well, it was now slightly yellowish. For that reason she said she was considering getting in touch with the out-of-hours service at Ards Hospital. Meanwhile, I judged that I could still make it to the morning service at Ballyhackamore. I had participated in this meeting consistently since becoming a member of the church as a boy of 16, but this was to be the last time I would attend on a Sunday morning.

When I returned home, I found Sandra speaking on the telephone with a doctor at the hospital. I listened as she explained her symptoms. While the doctor initially seemed reluctant to see her, he did, in the end, ask her to go down. We left promptly without eating the lunch that Sandra had prepared for me.

Once more, we found ourselves sitting anxiously in a hospital waiting room. However, we were seen reasonably quickly and this time the doctor's reaction was different. Having had the benefit of seeing Sandra, and anxious about her condition, he sympathetically declared that he would want to see her again if she was a *relative* of

---

[11] James 4:14 (NIV)

his. He then proceeded to write a letter which we were to take immediately to the Ulster Hospital A&E. He warned us that he was painting a serious picture, but asked us not to be alarmed as he just wanted to ensure that his medical colleagues were fully aware of Sandra's recent symptoms. Sandra plainly asked, "Doctor, have I got cancer?" He responded by saying that he couldn't see inside her, but that the Ulster Hospital would conduct all the necessary tests. We returned straight home to collect some clothes as we both knew that it was now very likely she would be kept in.

Weather wise, it was such a pleasant summer's afternoon as we drove once more to the Ulster Hospital. The television in A&E was covering the Open golf championship (which Rory McIlroy went on to win). Sandra lifted her weary eyes towards the screen and said, "How is Rory doing?" A feel good factor would be experienced by many folk across Northern Ireland later that evening, but for us that was a million miles away; my mind was swirling.

Jaundice is caused by the build up of bilirubin in the blood. Initial tests confirmed that the level in Sandra's blood was high, and so, as expected, she would not be allowed to go home. "Mum has to stay, Son" I advised Edward over the phone. He and Anna arrived just as Sandra was being admitted. At long last, after almost two months of discomfort and numerous consultations with several doctors, Sandra was finally in the hospital. I went home that Sunday evening reassured that she was now going to be thoroughly examined.

Many members of the family gathered somewhat spontaneously at Sandra's mum's house in Dundonald. We talked optimistically about how Sandra would surely receive the treatment necessary to restore her to health and strength again. Life would surely be back to normal quite soon. However, Sandra texted early on Monday morning to tell me of her dreadful night with pain in her back, and lovingly added, *'Hope you had a better nite lol x.'* She then texted again later to let me know that a consultant had called to see her and had confirmed that a scan was being arranged. *'No long waiting anymore Love x,'* I replied.

As it happened, I had booked annual leave for that day (Monday, 21st July) because the little log cabin we had ordered was to be erected in the back garden. I thought it best to be at home when the builders arrived. When they did, I advised them that my wife had been admitted to the hospital quite suddenly the previous day, and that I would be leaving to visit her after lunch. The sun was shining and it was such a perfect day for the job. My thoughts, however, were very much elsewhere.

When I arrived at the hospital Sandra seemed a little more upbeat and Ward 5 had experienced 'a night with Sandra' despite her pain and discomfort. "We had quite a night ladies, didn't we?" she announced, with her usual gusto. A CT scan was scheduled for that afternoon, and despite being anxious, she joked about the large jug of water sitting in front of her that would have to be taken beforehand. After months of waiting it seemed like everything was now moving very quickly, and sure enough, the porters soon arrived to take Sandra for this all-important scan. "I'll be back at 7pm to see how you got on," I told her as the lift doors opened and she was whisked away.

I was back home around 4pm and the log cabin was almost constructed. I had sent Sandra a photograph earlier in the day when it had been half built, but now it looked great, though uninspiring, given the circumstances. I struggled to show any degree of enthusiasm. Friends often pay a compliment about its appearance, but I sadly reflect on the fact that it was built on one of the worst day of my life. When I open the kitchen blinds each morning and notice it, its very presence gently whispers, *'Remember 21st July 2014?'*

My dad, a joiner by trade, called that afternoon to see the cabin being built. After he went home, I decided to eat some of Sunday's dinner – still in the oven and untouched – before returning to the hospital. I sat down in the living room. It was 5.45pm. Just then the phone rang. It was Sandra. How many thousands of times I had lifted the phone and heard her voice... *'What are you up to?'*; *'Where is Edward?'*;

'What are we having for tea?'; 'How did West Ham do today?'; 'I'm on the bus now so just pick me up at 6.30pm' ...but not this time! "The Doctors want to talk to both of us together, Love, so can you come up to the hospital now?" I froze. I felt sick.

Almost 31 years earlier I had made that wonderful phone call that would ultimately lead to marriage, but now I was receiving a phone call from Sandra that would signal the beginning of the end of our precious relationship. I set the plate of food on the kitchen table and somehow drove to the Ulster Hospital. I knew that the only reason for such a hasty appointment with the consultants had to be to convey bad news; but how bad was it going to be? I tried to think positively, but it was so horribly difficult. I prayed to the Lord for help.

Upon arriving at Ward 5 we were both taken to the Sister's office where two consultants and a nurse were waiting. Their ashen faces said it all, even before they started to discuss Sandra's condition. "This is much more serious than we thought!" the senior consultant declared. Sandra had a tumour. It was a cancer of the pancreas. That 'C' word is frightening, but so much more chilling when it's accompanied by the word pancreatic.

My mouth was dry, and I struggled to speak. I asked how this could possibly be considering that Sandra's ultra scan at the Downe Hospital just three weeks earlier had shown her pancreas to be 'not remarkable'. Replying with great sensitivity, the consultant explained that ultra scans were limited in what they are able to reveal. I could see that he was visibly upset as he discussed the extent of Sandra's cancer. Surgery would not be possible since the cancer had spread to her liver.

I longed for a glimmer of light and dared to suggest chemotherapy or radiotherapy – anything at all, but I detected little or no enthusiasm for either. In a heartfelt attempt to support us, the consultant added, "We will make Sandra comfortable." The word

Sandra aged 3 months with her mum, grandmother and aunt Alice

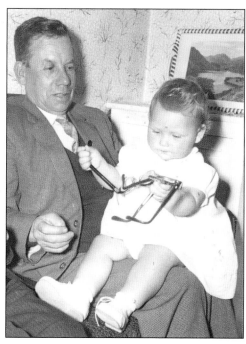

Sandra with her grandfather

A visit to Santa with her sister, Linda

Sisters

*Sandra during
her primary
school days*

*Sandra appointed Form Captain at
Dundonald Girls High School*

'Sandy' toasting the Great Southern Hotels summer holiday offers in July 1980 while working for Arcadia Travel

'Sandy' working for AA Travel

'Sandy' with AA Director-General, Mr O.F. Lambert, and AA Area Manager for
Northern Ireland, Mr J.V. McConnell, on 25th June 1987

Together at church youth camp in Dublin in July 1984

With Samuel and Linda on the Greek island of Rhodes during our first holiday together in July 1984

*Our wedding
at the Iron
Hall,
Templemore
Avenue,
Belfast, on
27th August
1986*

*"Let the
congregation
be seated"*

The signing of the marriage register with Pastor Jack Mitchell

Enjoying the blessing of parents

Looking ahead to our future together

Sandra with my mum, March 1987

Sandra with her mum, dad and Linda during a visit to the Ulster American Folk Park, Omagh, on 10th September 1988

*Edward is
born on
14th September
1989*

Sandra, and Edward, at her grandmother's 80th birthday party on 12th January 1991

'Sandy' having dinner aboard the Bateaux Mouches while cruising along the River Seine as a guest of the Paris Travel Service during a Thomas Cook educational trip to the French capital in April 1997

Visiting Paris with our neice Emma in July 1997

Priceless memories of Florida with nephew John (June-July 2003) and nieces Anne-Louise (July 2004) and Naomi (August 2005)

At the Magic Kingdom, Disney World, Florida in August 2005

Edward with his mum at Times Square, New York in June 2009

Sandra with her mum and stepdad, Sammy

Sandra and Linda at Anne-Louise's wedding on 22nd April 2011

'comfortable' sounded strange in such distressing circumstances. To hear it was cancer was horrendous, but to be told, in effect, that it was terminal, was much too difficult to grasp. However, Sandra, to reassure those in the room, bravely declared, "I'm in God's hands now."

On 26th September 2006 my dad had been rushed to the Ulster Hospital with similar pain and had been diagnosed with pancreatitis. When being discharged on 6th October, Sandra sat with him as the consultant explained that a pancreatic tumour could not be ruled out at that stage. Subsequent numerous scans, however, resulted in him being given the 'all clear'. Now, just over seven years later, Sandra sat in the same hospital discussing her own pancreas, but this time the prognosis could not have been more different.

What had been the worst few minutes of our lives ended, and mercifully, Sandra was not taken back into the open bay in Ward 5. Nurses considerately escorted us to one of the more private sideward's along the corridor in Ward 6. We were so very grateful for this. It was now 7pm, and being visiting time, our nieces Anne-Louise and Emma arrived. Their initial smiles were quickly replaced by tears. "Phone your mum and nanny and tell them to come up to the hospital," I said. Soon the little sideward was a scene of unrelenting heartache.

A few hours earlier I had *received* the most devastating phone call of my life and now I had to *make* the most difficult phone call of my life. I had to call Edward and ask him to come to the hospital once he had finished his shift delivering online shopping for Sainsbury's. I tried to speak calmly, as I was conscious that he may have been driving his van, and I obviously didn't want to alarm him. It truly broke Edward's heart when he came into the sideward just after 9pm and his mum told him the dreadful news. It was an unimaginable moment. Anna's mum, Lynn, arrived a short time later and shared in our distress. She happened to be at the hospital as her dad had also been admitted that day.

I was very grateful that evening when asked if I wanted to sleep on the floor beside Sandra. So, after our loved ones had gone home to cry, and the staff had gone to carry out their other duties, a mattress was brought from the store on the other side of the corridor. We tried to comprehend the enormity of the previous few hours. Was this all a dream? Surely this wasn't really happening. We tried to sleep, but oh, the restlessness and anguish. At daybreak the light shone in to that little room, but it couldn't penetrate our darkness. It was unbearable to even begin contemplating living without Sandra, and yet, I wondered what Sandra was really thinking.

It's strange how life seems to go on as normal, even in the surroundings of a hospital where sickness and death are so close at hand. The mattress had to be put back in the store when the nurses brought in medicine and some breakfast for Sandra. I knew that, somehow, I needed to personally tell relatives and friends of this devastating diagnosis. I couldn't just phone, or text, or leave it to others. So, I made my way back to the home we had shared throughout our married life. I looked around, and yes, it was the same semi-detached bungalow with the furniture sitting as it was the previous day. However, the rooms were now 'cold and empty'. Without Sandra's presence, I knew it was no more than bricks and mortar. My stay there was brief since I quickly left to tell my mum and dad, my sister Hilary, and my Aunt Joan. Understandably, they were stunned. Then it was back to the hospital.

I was transfixed by such surreal circumstances. I couldn't hold back the tears. Sometimes these flowed gently as I sat speechless with Sandra and the rest of the family. At other times, when away from everyone, I wailed as never before. One such occasion was while driving towards Jim's house. Jim, his wife Jackie, and their little daughter, Brooke, had also attended the small Christian fellowship at Ballyhackamore and had shared so many of the responsibilities there with us. We valued their friendship, too, and enjoyed Sunday evening suppers in their home. Little Brooke often sought out Sandra on Sunday mornings for her customary hug.

Sadly, Jackie died of cancer on 19th May 2013 and her death brought much sadness to everyone in the church. I was greatly honoured to have been asked to pray at her graveside. I confessed to Jim at that time that I couldn't fully appreciate the depth of his sorrow since I had never walked in his shoes. But on this occasion, I wanted him to know of Sandra's diagnosis and of how that I was *now* walking in his shoes. He could in a very real way identify with the burden that I was carrying.

Back in hospital, Sandra was trying to remain focused. She informed me that she didn't want to cry as she believed it would do her little good. The angelic-like nurses treated her with unimaginable care as she continued to smile and laugh with them. She boldly declared to them, "We gotta fight, fight, fight, fight, fight..." [12] words from a familiar pop song that typified her indomitable spirit –

> *Anything that's worth having,*
> *Is sure enough worth fighting for,*
> *Quiting's out of the question,*
> *When it gets tough, gotta fight some more.*

She then asked those nurses, "But how do you fight?"

Sandra would go on to fight with every ounce of her dwindling energy, and with such steely determination, but this wasn't going to be a fair fight as was evident much sooner than I could ever have imagined.

---

[12] https://en.wikipedia.org/wiki/Fight_for_This_Love

'Remember him before the silver cord is
severed, and the golden bowl is broken;
before the pitcher is shattered at the spring,
and the wheel broken at the well,
and the dust returns to the ground it came from,
and the spirit returns to God who gave it.' [13]

CHAPTER 6

The Fragility of Life

Each day during the week that Sandra was diagnosed largely followed the same pattern, and yet, much of it remains a blur. We tried to sleep at night but basically just tossed and turned until the hospital's morning routine brought the long weary hours to an end. One incident, however, stands out with great fondness. Sandra had noticed that the sheet supplied with my mattress had fallen to the floor, so she tenderly leaned down from her bed and pulled it back over me. Despite her discomfort, she never stopped showing that unwavering love and care for me. My heart was breaking; I felt so powerless to help her in return.

Following breakfast, we would wait anxiously, yet optimistically, for the consultant to come and give us news regarding possible treatment. With the human heart being what it is, we longed for a glimmer of hope. I wanted to know more about Sandra's illness and yet, at the same time, I didn't. In the weeks leading up to this, as previously mentioned, I had scoured the NHS website for information about the various cancers; the symptoms, the prognosis,

---

[13] Ecclesiastes 12:6-7 (NIV)

etc., but now I was frightened to read any more, or indeed, ask too many questions.

After the consultant had done his morning rounds I would routinely go home to shower and change clothes before returning to the hospital for the remainder of the day. Relatives, and just one or two close friends, visited Sandra each day. However, I felt obliged to text the countless friends listed on Sandra's phone and explain that she was too ill for visits. I'm confident that the hospital's extensive car parking facilities would have been insufficient, should they have all arrived together!

On Wednesday, 23rd July, the consultant explained that at the multidisciplinary team meeting it had been decided to carry out a procedure the following Friday. As often happens, Sandra's pancreatic cancer had put pressure on her bile duct, which caused a blockage, and hence, jaundice. The condition leads to a general feeling of sickness, loss of appetite and tiredness. Consequently, it may be necessary to place a stent into the bile duct to allow the bile to flow into the bowel to reduce the symptoms. During the planned procedure, 'scrapings' were also to be taken in an attempt to ascertain the exact type of pancreatic cancer Sandra was suffering from. This would, at least to some degree, dictate the treatment options as far as chemotherapy was concerned.

Pancreatic cancers are divided it two main groups – exocrine and endocrine. Exocrine tumours start in the exocrine cells where digestive enzymes are made and account for approximately 95% of tumours. The most common of these is pancreatic ductal adenocarcinomas (PDAC's). Endocrine tumours (also called neuroendocrine tumours), on the other hand, start in the hormone producing cells in the pancreas and make up less than 5% of the cancers. I will comment further in Chapter 10.

Friday's procedure took place as planned, and coupled with new medication, an improvement was clearly noticeable the following day. Her pain had eased and she had a much healthier complexion. There was some emotional respite. I wondered if this was to be a turning point for the better.

Sandra informed me on the Saturday afternoon that one of the nurses treating her was getting married, and that that day was to be her last at work before the wedding. "You will need to go to Warden's in Newtownards and buy a wedding present," she declared in such a matter of fact way. I was surprised at how rational and caring she was despite her personal circumstances. Sandra was so physically weak, and yet withal, her inert interest in others, and her desire to give, never waned. Buying wedding presents would always have been Sandra's 'department', so my discussing the options with the sales representative was very strange.

The following day, Sunday, bore no resemblance whatsoever to typical Sundays for us. Monday came – exactly one week after the diagnosis – and we were informed that Sandra could go home while the consultants waited for her test results. I was dreading this moment. There was a degree of comfort by having Sandra in the care of professional hospital staff. After all, what did I know about managing her pain? Before we left though, I turned to her as she lay in bed, and said, "Smile Love – this has been our 'hotel room' for the past week!" and took a photograph.

That remarkable image, taken with a very basic mobile phone, would be the last photograph of my Sandra. No 'air brushing' or 'make up' was required. She just did not look ill. It reflected an inner peace and serenity that spoke more powerfully of the reality of the Christian faith than any sermon I had ever preached. That photo occupies a prominent place in the hall and study at home; my office desk at work and at the front of the Bible that Sandra bought me all those years ago. It also adorns the homes of so many of her family and friends.

As we arrived home in Saratoga Avenue later that Monday afternoon there was a pleasant surprise awaiting Sandra; one that lifted her spirits. When she had left for the hospital a week earlier the house was in a bit of a mess due to the refurbishment work. However, the scene was now reminiscent of the television show, 'DIY SOS', as Edward, Anna, Paul (Anna's dad), William (Anna's brother), Peter (Edward's Best Man) and not forgetting Stephen (a decorator who had kindly cancelled other jobs to help) were all working tirelessly to put the place back into some kind of order for Sandra's homecoming; the hall and living room were freshly painted, a large cosy rug complemented new curtains, the suite so excitedly ordered at Easter had arrived and was complemented with new cushions. Sandra smiled in grateful appreciation.

We tried our best to live normally that week as the family gathered at our home on Tuesday and Wednesday for dinner, and to spend precious time together. Sadly, this lull didn't last long because the consultant called us to say that he wanted Sandra back in hospital on Thursday for a liver biopsy. Apparently, the scrapings taken during the earlier procedure had been inconclusive. Disappointed, it was back to the Ulster, and this time to Ward 8 where a nurse disclosed to us that the consultant had been adamant that 'a bed must be found for Mrs Carson'. Sandra seemed to have touched his heart; I knew he was trying his very best to do everything possible to help her.

The bed was in a large room at the end of Ward 8 and once again, I was permitted to stay overnight. I recall how at suppertime the ancillary nurse enquired if we wanted tea and toast. This nurse appeared uncharacteristically tetchy. Apologising, she explained that her daughter had recently gone blind due to diabetes and that she was hoping that an urgent request to take early retirement would be approved. I could see the tears suddenly well up in Sandra's eyes. Apologetically, the nurse told Sandra that it had not been her intention to upset her. Again, that incident spoke volumes. Sandra still shared in the grief of others during her own darkest of days.

On Friday, 1st August, we sat together and waited for the porters to come and take Sandra to theatre. As we did so, Sandra found comfort in her Bible reading that morning; *'...the LORD sustains them on their sickbed and restores them from their bed of illness.'* [14]

With the theatre procedure over, and the consultant very pleased, I was able to go home that evening. However, when I rang Sandra's phone at almost 11pm I worryingly received no answer. Then a text came through at 0.30am, *'Sorry I've slept until just now lol luv u my Gary xxx.'* What a precious text message.

Sandra was permitted to leave the hospital again on Saturday, so Edward and Anna joined us at home for tea. They accompanied us, too, on Sunday afternoon as we went to visit Mervyn and Pamela. How many happy times we had spent in each other's homes and on holiday over the years, including the Mediterranean cruise just ten months earlier, but this brief visit to Mervyn and Pamela was to be our last.

The week that followed was the final full week Sandra and I spent together at our home. She tried so very hard to keep on fighting and supporting me in my emotional turmoil. As we read the Bible and prayed together, I wished we had done so much more often when life had been normal. We cried to the Lord for healing as countless others did in churches across the country. Sandra took heart knowing that so many other Christians were also praying for her healing.

We watched a few TV programmes together and one of our favourite films, the rather unfamiliar love story, *'The Student Prince'*. Somehow, I wanted us both to sit and cry again in the way that we did while watching it so many times before. The last scene had always invoked tears when the Prince referred to his sweetheart as "My only Love", and her responding with, "Your first Love." Those words became jovial greetings between us over the years.

Sandra was adamant that the house refurbishment work should continue. Therefore, a new stair carpet was fitted while the installation of the worktops went ahead in the kitchen. We had been

---

[14] Psalm 41:3 (NIV)

so excited about these new granite tops, but that excitement had now died. To think, that in a matter of months the choice of a marble headstone would occupy my mind instead.

While family did visit us, Sandra still made every possible effort to call with them. On Tuesday, 5th August, we went to Edward and Anna's for tea. Sandra was so very proud of them, and of the work they undertook the previous year to turn the rather neglected house that they had purchased into a beautiful home. But again, this was to be another in this series of 'last times'.

On the Thursday evening, we went back to Donaghadee for a short drive and sat along the seafront. I encouraged Sandra to eat some chips, but she had no appetite. She became generally disinterested, and so we were soon on the road home.

On the following Saturday afternoon Sandra ventured out with me again. We parked the car in Newtownards town centre and took a few steps towards Warden's. However, we soon realised that she simply couldn't go any further and had to return to the car. Sandra's strength was rapidly failing in front of my eyes. Still, she managed to call at my mum and dad's house and Linda and Samuel's house, that afternoon – again, for the last time.

Sunday, 10th August, dawned. It was just three weeks to the day that Sandra had been admitted to the Ulster Hospital and she had one last home to visit. It was to Anna's mum and dad's where we had been invited for dinner. That afternoon will live long in the memory of everyone sitting around the table. Sandra calmly rose to her feet after the meal, and addressing Edward, bravely declared that he had a good dad and a good wife, who, along with Anna's family, would look after him when she was gone. Understandably, we wept.

Sadly, Sandra was back in the Ulster Hospital two days later. She had wakened up with double vision and was advised by her own doctor to go straight back to A&E where they undertook a CT scan of her brain. While telling us that everything seemed OK, it was suggested that she could stay until the next day to avail of an MRI scan. She was duly admitted to Ward 15.

I went home that evening and returned to the hospital the following morning just before Sandra was taken for the scan. Remaining motionless for over 30 minutes during such a renowned claustrophobic procedure would be Sandra's worst nightmare. I thought of her panic during a ride at Disneyworld when a harness was placed over her head. I prayed that the Lord would keep her calm during the process, which He did. I was most thankful that she had not pressed the button to exit the machine.

When I asked Sandra how she managed to cope during the scan she replied that she had spent the time meditating upon Isaiah Chapter 6 and one of my sermons concerning it. She had listened to this a number of times over the years and it is fair to say that she understood the key points every bit as well as me. The verses in question recorded the testimony of the prophet Isaiah who said, '*In the year that King Uzziah died, I saw also the Lord, sitting upon a throne, high and lifted up, and his train filled the temple.*' [15] Sandra, too, would see the Lord much sooner than either of us realised that afternoon.

We waited patiently for the results, and after several hours were again relieved to hear that everything was apparently clear. Sandra could again go home, although we were instructed to go to the Eye Clinic at the Royal Victoria Hospital (RVH), Belfast the following day. So, on Thursday morning Edward and Linda accompanied us there for further tests. The practitioners explained that the double vision may have been due to a small blood vessel having burst, but they did not seem overly concerned. They intimated that they would see Sandra again in a fortnight or so. Sandra, by now availing of a wheelchair, was becoming weaker as each moment passed. Upon entering the hospital café, she immediately asked to leave, as she could no longer tolerate the smell of cooked food or even coffee.

---

[15] Isaiah 6:1 (KJV)

Later that evening, Sandra's manager and another colleague from her Thomas Cook days called to see her at home. I gently wakened her and she promptly put on her dressing gown before going to the living room. She greeted her visitors by exclaiming, "John, Sharon, I'm sure you didn't expect to see me like this!" Despite her discomfort, she conversed as only she could, and enquired about *their* general wellbeing.

When we had arrived home from the RVH earlier that day, a message on the telephone answering machine informed us that Sandra's consultant wanted to see her again the following day regarding the results of the liver biopsy. Sandra was very tired after three days of being in and out of hospital, but agreed to attend.

Next morning I helped get Sandra ready for the appointment. She was now reaching the very end in terms of physical strength. Sitting on the bottom of the stairs, she sighed and said, "I can't do this anymore Love." I pleaded with her to try, as that day might have brought her some news about chemotherapy. Edward arrived to accompany us to the hospital, and somehow, Sandra managed to make her way to the car and back to Ward 6 of the Ulster Hospital. The consultant confirmed that Sandra had pancreatic adenocarcinoma – the most common form of pancreatic cancer, as already stated – and that the Oncology Department at the City Hospital's Cancer Centre would be in touch to discuss chemotherapy. The word 'treatment' had always sounded positive, and while I stubbornly refused to give up hope, it was now becoming increasingly difficult to be optimistic.

It has been said that *'people don't care what you say until they know you care'*. In the depths of her own suffering Sandra still cared. During her first week in hospital, the consultant had told Sandra that he had fallen and hurt his back, so Sandra being Sandra, took the opportunity to ask him how he was feeling. Trivialising his own condition, he replied, "Oh, I'm OK." As we left those wonderful nurses that had treated Sandra so lovingly during her previous stay, surrounded her and graciously tried to assure her that she was looking well. On the surface, she still was, but Sandra masked much of her pain.

We drove straight to Sandra's mum and stepdad's home – just a mile away in Dundonald – to tell them that chemotherapy was to be discussed with the City Hospital. But Sandra was wilting fast. I turned to her and said, "You're not well Love, really not well, and I'm going to call an ambulance." 999 brought an ambulance within a couple of minutes. As I sat beside her on the way back to the Ulster Hospital I could see the medics become increasingly concerned. She barely responded when they spoke her name. More worryingly, I then saw her arm fall to the side.

Upon arrival at the hospital, Sandra was swiftly taken away. I sat with Edward and Linda in A&E truly dreading any news. It was the longest wait; probably just less than an hour, but it felt like an eternity. A doctor eventually came and broke the news to us that Sandra had had a serious stroke. I immediately walked outside to where the ambulances were parked. I seemed unable to cope with anything more. Surely not a stroke on top of everything else, I lamented.

I quickly returned, though, and asked how this could have happened. The doctor explained that pancreatic cancer can cause the blood to thicken, and this, in turn, can lead to blood clots. [Apparently patients with pancreatic cancer, especially those with advanced or metastatic cancer (cancer that has spread beyond a particular organ to other parts of the body) are at higher risk of deep vein thrombosis (DVT).] Blood clots had travelled to Sandra's brain and caused an ischaemic stroke. They also had gone to her lungs, causing a pulmonary embolism. Sandra had no power on her right-hand side and was now critically ill.

The doctors did not offer any hope of recovery. One explained the extent of Sandra's stroke. I struggled with her seemingly abrupt comment, "Do you understand what I am saying?" Edward sought

to reassure me by saying, "She is just trying to prepare you, Dad."
I suppose it was a case of being cruel to be kind. I was also warned
that it was unlikely Sandra would be able to swallow again or even
speak.

I found it terribly difficult accepting the decision not to transfer
Sandra to the Intensive Care Unit (ICU) or give her any form of
resuscitation due to the cancer prognosis. It all seemed very unfair
as Sandra was moved to Ward 23 showing very few signs of
consciousness.

Nevertheless, the doctors gave Sandra one dose of a clot-busting
medication and not long afterwards, to the amazement of the entire
family now gathered at her bedside, she took a glass of water and
began to speak a little. She even managed to lift herself up on the
bed. I wept when I saw that one of the nurses on duty that evening
was a lovely Christian girl who had once been in Sandra's Sunday
school class. She lived just opposite Ballyhackamore Gospel Hall. I
said to Sandra, "You know Sarah, don't you Love?" Sandra uttered,
"Yes, from across the road." These were the last words I recall Sandra
speaking. How comforting it is to know that Sarah cared for Sandra
during those final few days of her life. It was as if God had placed
Sarah there. Surely it was another 'God incident'.

Being well past midnight, I eventually went to lie down in the Relatives
Room while Sandra slept. However, at 6am that Saturday morning, a
nurse wakened me to tell me that Sandra had once again lost power
on her right side and was to be taken for further scans. I walked beside
Sandra's bed as she was taken down the corridor and then waited
outside the room. Scans subsequently revealed that Sandra's condition
had deteriorated after those initial encouraging signs.

By Sunday afternoon Sandra had been taken to a sideward. As we sat
with her, the door happened to be open and I noticed a good friend
walk past. It was Drew Craig, a man whom I held in the highest
esteem, not only as a Bible teacher but also as my boss during the

mid 1980s while working at Stormont. I rose to my feet immediately and pursued him as he made his way to visit an elderly member of his own fellowship. As we embraced, Drew said, "Oh Gary, before I left the house I just asked the Lord if I could possibly meet you." In the stillness of that open corridor, he read a verse from the Scriptures with me in an attempt to provide some solace in the dark situation in which I found myself. (He would read this verse again when speaking at Sandra's Thanksgiving Service.) He asked if he could pray with Sandra at her bedside, and as he did so, Sandra reverently closed her eyes.

Sandra was still determined to fight for life and remarkably began to eat and drink again. It was just a little at a time, but I reckoned that eating anything at all was surely good. As the family sat round the bed each of us took it in turn to sit close to her and hold her hand. I persistently looked for any slight movement on her right side and urged her to keep on fighting.

Each day that week began with phone calls to Edward and Sandra's mum to update them on how Sandra had been during the night, before they would leave home for the hospital. Meanwhile, I was routinely encouraged to go to the Relatives Room while the nursing staff attended to Sandra. As I sat in that room visitors enquired if my mum had been admitted, and I can recall that look of amazement on their faces when I informed them it was *my wife* who was gravely ill. Sandra looked so terribly out of place with so many patients nearby in their elderly years.

As darkness descended each evening I lay down on the floor beside Sandra. I had done so at the time of the original diagnosis, but this now was very different. We could no longer have those intimate chats. How distressing it is when the one you love so much loses the power to speak.

The hours of night passed slowly and the place felt so desolate. A blanket draped forlornly over the curtain pole in an attempt to close out the light. A nurse apologised for the lack of curtains and window blinds, adding that this had been reported some time earlier but due to financial constraints it was still on the 'To do' list. In all honesty, it didn't matter in the slightest, and yet it was striking as I lay there contrasting it with the beautiful cabin that we had so recently shared on the Mediterranean cruise ship. The differences were extreme.

Anytime Sandra moved, I would jump up and check her oxygen mask. I awoke around 5am on the Wednesday morning – just six days after her stroke – and again fixed the mask. This time, she wrapped her left arm around me and held me. It was such a precious moment that will remain with me forever.

Later that morning Sandra took porridge and coffee, and something further at lunchtime. Hope resurfaced. However, by late afternoon I had an awful feeling that Sandra was again struggling. Her breathing seemed more laboured, yet she tried to eat again at teatime. I was once more encouraged to go to the Relatives Room and thus took the opportunity to eat some food which Sandra's mum had brought for me. I then went down to the entrance hall to purchase a drink. Suddenly, my mobile rang. It was Anna requesting me to return urgently as the nurses had observed Sandra becoming very agitated. I ran upstairs and as I entered the sideward I could see Sandra gasping for each breath. My beloved Sandra was unable to fight any more. I pleaded with the medical team, "Please do something. Please don't let my Sandra go." With that, the nurse by her side gently whispered just three agonizing words, "Your Sandra's gone."

We were immersed in grief, tears and unfathomable sorrow. How could this possibly have happened so quickly? We lingered in disbelief before I finally knelt beside my Sandra, gave thanks to God for my darling wife, and prayed again for help. Somehow, we all eventually managed to leave. I took my dad back to his home and broke the news to my frail mum. I retreated to Linda's house and sent out the saddest text I ever had to send, informing everyone that Sandra had been 'called Home'. Edward and Anna then took me to their home in Donaghadee where I curled up in Edward's little study room. I was now alone and inconsolable.

On 20th July 2014 Sandra had been admitted to the Ulster Hospital for those exploratory tests and then given the terrible diagnosis the following day. Now, exactly one month later, on 20th August 2014, Sandra was gone.

I have often used the expression *'I lost my wife'* but in truth, I haven't lost her. You only lose something if you don't know where it is. I knew where Sandra was. But that didn't ease the pain in my aching heart that night as death, *'the last enemy'*, [16] separated us after almost 28 years of marriage.

---

[16]   1 Corinthians 15: 26 (KJV)

'Sarah...died...and Abraham came to mourn for Sarah, and to weep for her. And after this Abraham buried Sarah his wife in the cave of the field of Machpelah before Mamre: the same is Hebron in the land of Canaan.' [17]

CHAPTER 7

The Unexpected Funeral

It had been my privilege to present the Christian gospel to children and adults in various churches since my late teens and in many a sermon I emphasised the sombre reality of death. When speaking of Christ's death upon the cross for the sin of the world, I often pointed out that the Latin word *Calvary*[18] signified the place of the skull. The skull is emblematic of death, and so prior to contemplating God's love for each of us we had to focus our minds on man's mortality. I reminded those present that life was indeed temporal and how that the Bible declared, *'It is appointed unto men once to die but after this the judgement.'* [19]

I occasionally quoted William Saroyan, the American novelist and playwright who, when facing death, said, "Everybody has got to die, but I have always believed an exception would be made in my case. Now what?" [20] If we are being honest, I suggest that many of us share his sentiments. We tend to think of death as applying only to others – perhaps older people and the ill. So, while I often spoke about

---

[17] Genesis 23:2,19 (KJV)
[18] Luke 23:33 (KJV)
[19] Hebrews 9:27 (KJV)
[20] https://www.goodreads.com/quotes/58517-everybody-has-got-to-die-but-i-have-always-believed

death, death generally did not preoccupy my mind. Yes, I knew about death theoretically, but not in a way that it radically affected my life.

Those formidable words, *'Till death us do part'* had been uttered sincerely during our marriage vows, but somehow, they seemed remote and scarcely worth thinking about on that blessed day back in August 1986. We had a lifetime ahead of us. Death was surely a long way down the road— something that would perhaps bring our latter years of nursing home care to an end. Strangely though, it felt like those vows had only just been spoken and yet death had now parted us. I struggled to accept that Sandra was really gone.

I will deal with the funeral in detail shortly, however it is important to state that while lying on the floor beside Sandra every night in the hospital, and despite the prognosis that her condition was terminal, I repeatedly dismissed the thought of it from my mind. I stubbornly held on to the Scripture that I had shared with Sandra, *'I will restore health…'* [21] Indeed, while sitting alone beside her during those last few days I also interpreted my Bible readings in such a way as to convince myself that Sandra would recover regardless of what I was being told.

My daily reading on the day following Sandra's stroke was taken from the Gospel of Mathew and included the following verses –

Early in the morning, as Jesus was on his way back to the city, he was hungry. Seeing a fig tree by the road, he went up to it but found nothing on it except leaves. Then he said to it, "May you never bear fruit again!" Immediately the tree withered. When the disciples saw this, they were amazed. "How did the fig tree wither so quickly?" they asked. Jesus replied, "Truly I tell you, if you have faith and do not doubt, not only can you do what was done to the fig tree, but also you can say to this mountain, Go, throw yourself into the sea, and it will be done. If you believe, you will receive whatever you ask for in prayer." [22]

[21] Jeremiah 30:17 (KJV)
[22] Mathew 21:18-27 (NIV)

My Scripture Union Bible reading notes added that, *'With God, anything is possible.'* Consequently, I would keep asking God for the impossible.

On the Sunday morning the reading notes took me to the Psalms –

I lift up my eyes to you, to you who sit enthroned in heaven. As the eyes of slaves look to the hand of their master, as the eyes of a female slave look to the hand of her mistress, so our eyes look to the LORD our God, till he shows us his mercy. [23]

The contributor added, *'Sometimes all you can do is wait. You lose your job unexpectedly; someone close to you is diagnosed with a terrible illness.'*

Yes, I would keep on waiting upon the Lord for his mercy and healing.

Most moving of all, however, was the reading on the day before Sandra died.[24] It was the account of how David had been anointed King of all Israel at the city of Hebron. While his royal headquarters was based there for some seven years, he still had his eyes on a new capital – the high rocky plateau of the Jebusites that had previously proved unassailable. What a challenge! It was surely too hard to capture. Verses 4 and 5 of I Chronicles 11 seemed to stand out –

David and all the Israelites marched to Jerusalem (that is, Jebus). The Jebusites who lived there said to David, "You will not get in here." Nevertheless, David captured the fortress of Zion – which is the City of David.

Against overwhelming odds the fortress of Zion was conquered, and I reckoned that, in like manner, Sandra would also pull through.

Those readings during the last few days of Sandra's life have often perturbed me. Yet, as I look back, I realise that the Lord did show

---

[23] Psalms 123:1-2 (NIV)
[24] 1 Chronicles 11: 1-9 (NIV)

mercy – but not as I had imagined. I trust that the Lord will help me understand those readings more fully one day. Meanwhile, as previously stated, I am now more conscious of the care needed not to apply verses out of context.

Just a few minutes after Sandra died I had hugged my dad in the hospital corridor and asked him disconsolately, "What am I going to do without my Sandra?" He replied, "You'll do what your Sandra would want you to do." So, as I wakened on 21st August 2014 – that dreadful first day without her – I knew I had to plan her funeral in a way that would honour both her and God. Those wise words of my father became a rock, and indeed, a compass in the years that have followed.

As I therefore began to plan a service of thanksgiving, there was only thing that I was actually sure of, and that was the hymns that we would sing. Sandra and I always agreed that our wedding hymns should be sung at our funerals too. But where would the service take place? Who would speak? Who would give a tribute? Where would Sandra be buried? What about refreshments for those attending? What insertions would be placed in the Belfast Telegraph? There were so many mind numbing questions that I never imagined having to face; at least not at the age of 51. And they were coming thick and fast.

The following morning, Edward, Anna and Anna's dad, Paul, accompanied me to S Clarke & Son, Funeral Directors in Newtownards and helped as I tried to make arrangements. Slowly, things began to take shape.

I had hoped that the service could be held in the Iron Hall, if at all possible, as this had been Sandra's spiritual home during her childhood and teenage years. It was also the place of our marriage. Thankfully, it was available on Saturday, 23rd August. Billy Brown, an elder who had such fond memories of Sandra as a young girl in the church, was the ideal person to chair the service. Arthur

Carnaghan – her close friend from the Iron Hall and former employer – would give a personal tribute as requested by Sandra in the latter days of her illness. He had given Sandra her first job in Travel, while their eldest daughter, Elizabeth, had been one of our bridesmaids.

I trusted that somehow I would receive the grace needed to pay my own tribute too. I simply had to. The speaker would be Drew Craig who had lovingly prayed with Sandra at the hospital. Immediately after I had made the arrangements with Drew, John Speirs, who had married Edward and Anna the previous year, telephoned to say that he intended travelling across from Scotland for the service. It was appropriate, therefore, to ask him to speak at the graveside.

As regards the cemetery, my thoughts turned to Ballyvester outside Donaghadee. It was close to Edward and Anna's new home, and where my grandparents and uncle were buried. We both had known it very well. A burial on the Saturday morning would be in order provided the cortege arrived by 11am.

The funeral directors then enquired as to the number of Order of Service sheets needed. I suggested at least 500. Somewhat taken aback, they pointed out that such a number could be excessive considering the early time of the service (9am) and the fact that many of our friends could be away on holiday since it was summertime. I assured them that the figure was a conservative estimate. They were not aware of the extent to which my Sandra was known. In the end, 500 were not enough! The front cover would feature a photograph of Sandra in the outfit that she wore to Edward and Anna's wedding just over a year earlier. She had looked so beautiful that day.

Of all the questions confronting me, one in particular sadly stands out: "What type of coffin do you want?" What a question! I thought of the countless occasions when, as a couple, we went selecting furniture together and debated the colours, the wood, the price and a host of other features, in this world of seemingly unlimited choice.

This was one piece of wood that I never imagined having to purchase.

Thursday brought so many decisions. It also brought visitors who came to share in our grief, and I will be forever grateful to those who worked tirelessly in Sandra's kitchen to provide hospitality. I continually chatted to folk, generally oblivious to all that was going on around me.

On Friday morning Edward and Anna took me to the cemetery to select a grave. As with the choosing of the coffin the previous day, it was surreal driving to Donaghadee to choose Sandra's grave, and inevitably, mine, too. I had often gone to tidy the graves of my grandparents, but never for a minute considered this journey.

As we travelled back to Newtownards, I sat quietly in the rear seat with a notebook and pen trying to jot down a few headings for my tribute. The Lord brought several to mind. So, upon returning home I withdrew to my small study, closed the door, and sought to draft Sandra's eulogy.

Right from our courtship days, Sandra had faithfully accompanied me when I was invited to speak at church services. I thought of the multitude of times she sat in the congregation giving her support as a wife, and of her countless words of support, and occasional, albeit justifiable, criticism. I never liked going without her, and she knew it. I would even dare to suggest that one or two invitations may have been based on the assumption that Sandra would be with me. Folks always enjoyed her company for supper afterwards. Typically, I would receive a phone call to confirm a booking and be asked, "Are you still OK to come on Sunday evening Gary?" followed by the words, "… and Sandra will be with you?" This eulogy would be for her, and in my heart of hearts I was convinced that this would be the last time I would speak from a church pulpit.

The funeral morning dawned with Edward and Anna being there to help me as the hearse arrived. Sandra's body had been brought back to the house and was now to be taken from it for a final time. It seemed such a short time since we had spotted the little bungalow for sale on Saratoga Avenue before excitedly moving in on our return from honeymoon. The neighbourhood felt eerily quiet as if everything was standing still in Sandra's honour.

The journey to the Iron Hall took less than 30 minutes. Again, I believe that it was no accident that a couple greeted me as I walked towards the door. They were Jackie and Audrey from Culcavy Hall. They had often invited both Sandra and me for supper when I was speaking at their church. They, too, had experienced heartache having lost their son, Gary, to cancer at the very young age of 21. Strangely, he and I shared the same birthday – 28th October, albeit 20 years apart. Their kind words at the entrance doors of the Iron Hall strengthened me.

My heart was overcome with immense pride as I saw the row of people lined along Templemore Avenue. The church was practically full notwithstanding it wasn't even 8.30am. Over 700 had gathered, making it, to the best of my knowledge, the largest funeral service that had been conducted in the new church building. The bright colours of travel agency uniforms lit up the building in the midst of the gloom.

The congregation heartily sang the two hymns sung at our wedding 28 years earlier in the former building. We had sung them so many times in the intervening years and I frequently selected them for services. That day they would be sung in solace, albeit in triumph too.

Loved with everlasting love [25]

Loved with everlasting love,
Led by grace that love to know;
Spirit, breathing from above,
Thou hast taught me it is so.

[25] George Wade Robinson (1838–1877)

Oh, this full and perfect peace!
Oh, this transport all divine!
In a love, which cannot cease,
I am His, and He is mine.

Heaven above is softer blue,
Earth around is sweeter green;
Something lives in every hue
Christless eyes have never seen:
Birds with gladder songs o'erflow,
Flow'rs with deeper beauties shine,
Since I know, as now I know,
I am His, and He is mine.

Things that once were wild alarms
Cannot now disturb my rest;
Closed in everlasting arms,
Pillowed on the loving breast.
Oh, to lie forever here,
Doubt and care and self resign,
While He whispers in my ear,
I am His, and He is mine.

His forever, only His:
Who the Lord and me shall part?
Ah, with what a rest of bliss
Christ can fill the loving heart.
Heaven and earth may fade and flee,
Firstborn light in gloom decline;
But, while God and I shall be,
I am His, and He is mine.

The sands of time are sinking [26]

The sands of time are sinking,
The dawn of Heaven breaks;
The summer morn I've sighed for –
The fair, sweet morn awakes:
Dark, dark hath been the midnight,
But dayspring is at hand,
And glory, glory dwelleth
In Immanuel's land.

(We omitted the opening verse at our wedding.)

O Christ, He is the fountain,
The deep, sweet well of love!
The streams on earth I've tasted
More deep I'll drink above:
There to an ocean fullness
His mercy doth expand,
And glory, glory dwelleth
In Immanuel's land.

With mercy and with judgment
My web of time He wove,
And aye, the dews of sorrow
Were lustred with His love;
I'll bless the hand that guided,
I'll bless the heart that planned
When throned where glory dwelleth
In Immanuel's land.

The bride eyes not her garment,
But her dear bridegroom's face;
I will not gaze at glory
But on my king of grace.

---

[26] Anne R. Cousin (1824–1906)

Not at the crown He giveth
But on His piercèd hand;
The Lamb is all the glory
Of Immanuel's land.

I've wrestled on towards Heaven,
Against storm and wind and tide,
Now, like a weary traveller
That leaneth on his guide,
Amid the shades of evening,
While sinks life's lingering sand,
I hail the glory dawning
From Immanuel's land.

In 2013, BBC's Songs of Praise conducted a nationwide survey of the most popular hymns in the UK in which tens of thousands of people voted. From a list of one hundred, the hymn *In Christ Alone* was ranked second only to *How Great Thou Art.* [27] This, too, seemed appropriate since it speaks unashamedly of the faith that Sandra had embraced as a child, and to which she held fervently throughout life, and significantly, as she faced death.

In Christ Alone [28]

In Christ alone my hope is found;
He is my light, my strength, my song;
This cornerstone, this solid ground,
Firm through the fiercest drought and storm.
What heights of love, what depths of peace,
When fears are stilled, when strivings cease!
My comforter, my all in all –
Here in the love of Christ I stand.

---

[27] http://www.bbc.co.uk/programmes/articles/3DnJQz7zsF1JrB3rZ8yQ86 w/the-uks-top-100-hymns
[28] Keith Getty & Stuart Townend (https://en.wikipedia.org/wiki/In_Christ_Alone)

In Christ alone, Who took on flesh,
Fullness of God in helpless babe!
This gift of love and righteousness,
Scorned by the ones He came to save.
Till on that cross as Jesus died,
The wrath of God was satisfied;
For ev'ry sin on Him was laid –
Here in the death of Christ I live.

There in the ground His body lay,
Light of the world by darkness slain;
Then bursting forth in glorious day,
Up from the grave He rose again!
And as He stands in victory,
Sin's curse has lost its grip on me;
For I am His and He is mine –
Bought with the precious blood of Christ.

No guilt in life, no fear in death –
This is the pow'r of Christ in me;
From life's first cry to final breath,
Jesus commands my destiny.
No pow'r of hell, no scheme of man,
Can ever pluck me from His hand;
Till He returns or calls me home –
Here in the pow'r of Christ I'll stand.

Arthur gave the first tribute. He expressed his family's love for Sandra dating back to those early days when she worked for him in Arcadia Travel and accompanied him on visits to hotels across the Irish Republic. He spoke of those occasions when he gave her a lift home and how they debated staying at home and putting their feet up, or going to the Bible study or Prayer meeting in the Iron Hall. Invariably they encouraged each other to attend the meetings. He reminisced about the babysitting years when she had first stayed overnight, and then weekends, and told of how their children were never content on Christmas Day until 'Auntie Sandra' arrived which showed that she was regarded as part of their family. Arthur spoke, too, of a loving person who went out of her way to please others and how she was the type of person whose company you always wanted to be in.

My turn came, and I rose to my feet. I hoped and prayed that, somehow, I could speak for ten precious minutes. My heart was broken, but I had to do this for my Sandra. Sheer determination seemed to suppress the raw emotion. I had stood on that very pulpit and preached several times, but again, had never envisaged this moment. Of the countless Get Well and Sympathy cards, one tiny card from Sandra's customers, Margaret and Jim, stood out. It would underpin what I had to say about the most wonderful person I had ever known. Written on the envelope that contained this card were the words, *'This little card just sums you up.'* The card read –

> *'Special' is a word that is used to describe something one of a kind, like a hug or a sunset or a person who spreads love with a smile or kind gesture. 'Special' describes people who act from the heart. 'Special' applies to something that is admired and precious and that can never be replaced. 'Special' is the word that best describes you.*

Yes, 'special' is a word often used, albeit sometimes, misused; but not so in Sandra's case. I reminded everyone, as if they needed reminding, that Sandra was indeed special. I spoke of her being a special travel consultant, a special friend, a special neighbour, a special aunt, a special niece, a special granddaughter, a special sister, a special daughter, a special daughter-in-law, a special mum (who had worn her 'Special Mum' necklace, that Edward bought her, with so much pride every day), a special wife, who had always affectionately called me 'My Gary', a special patient and a special Christian.

Drew then gave the address and read the same verses that he had shared with me in the corridor of Ward 23 the previous Sunday afternoon –

Dear friends, do not be surprised at the fiery ordeal that has come on you to test you, as though something strange were happening to you. But rejoice inasmuch as you participate in the sufferings of Christ, so that you may be overjoyed when his glory is revealed.[29]

After leaving me that Sunday, Drew had sought assurance from the Scriptures and on the following day, Monday, 18th August, found comfort in his daily devotional Bible reading notes and shared these also –

In all their affliction he was afflicted, and the angel of his presence saved them: in his love and in his pity he redeemed them; and he bare them, and carried them all the days of old.[30]

The contributor of those notes had added the following comments –

What a strange statement. How mysteriously wonderful? "In all their affliction he was afflicted." To think that the eternal God sympathises with the hurts and afflictions done to His people! The cries of Israel moved Him. Thank God, He knows and feels our every pain. He was tried in all points as we are, uniquely without sin, and therefore we have one who can sympathise with the feeling of our infirmities (Hebrews 4:15). No matter how dark the valley or difficult the way, we have "the angel of His presence" caring and guiding!

Drew handed me those treasured notes. Sandra would have been so glad to know that he spoke of her Saviour and His cross, His sufferings; His death and His resurrection when reassuring everyone present that she was now *'present with the Lord'*. Drew challenged the congregation by asking if they, too, were ready to face death. In closing, he quoted the words of another wonderful hymn – [31]

And is it so – I shall be like Thy Son?
Is this the grace which He for me has won?
Father of glory (thought beyond all thought!) –
In glory, to His own blest likeness brought!

---

[29] I Peter 4:12-13 (NIV)
[30] Isaiah 63:9 (KJV)
[31] John Nelson Darby (1800–1882)

Oh, Jesus, Lord, who loved me like to Thee?
Fruit of Thy work, with Thee, too, there to see
Thy glory, Lord, while endless ages roll,
Myself the prize and travail of Thy soul.

Yet it must be: Thy love had not its rest
Were Thy redeemed not with Thee fully blest.
That love that gives not as the world, but shares
All it possesses with its loved co-heirs.

Nor I alone; Thy loved ones all, complete
In glory, round Thee there with joy shall meet,
All like Thee, for Thy glory like Thee, Lord,
Object supreme of all, by all adored.

The heart is satisfied; can ask no more
All thought of self is now forever o'er:
Christ, its un-mingled object, fills the heart
In blest adoring love – the endless part.

Father of mercies, in Thy presence bright
All this shall be unfolded in the light;
Thy children all, with joy Thy counsels know
Fulfilled; patient in hope, while here below.

Kenneth Page, a lifelong friend, and elder at Ballyhackamore Gospel Hall, closed in prayer. He referred to the Christian hope that was our sure expectation – not mere wishful thinking – and that we would be together again with Sandra, and with her Saviour and Lord. He gave thanks to God for our memories of Sandra, who was *'so kind and so caring'*, who *'brought a smile to us'*, who had a *'happy, loving and bubbly* personality', whose *'greetings were gushing'*, who spoke with *'gusto and exuberant enthusiasm'*, whose *'touch was warm'* and whose *'hugs were all embracing'*.

The service ended, and when outside, I purposely stood alone for a few minutes before carrying Sandra's coffin a short distance along

Templemore Avenue. We then made our way to Ballyvester Cemetery for the committal conducted by John Speirs. Jim Peden closed in prayer. I had prayed at the graveside of Jim's wife, Jackie, just a year earlier; now he was praying at the grave of my beloved Sandra.

At a funeral service which I attended a number of years earlier, Drew Craig spoke about the death and burial of Sarah, the wife of the ancient patriarch Abraham. Abraham had buried her *'In the cave in the field of Machpelah'*. [32] Drew pointed out on that occasion that the name *Machpelah* meant 'double' and highlighted the fact that it indicated a place having double doors; that is, one with 'a way in' and 'a way out'. In other words, death was not the end for Abraham's Sarah, and neither was it for my Sandra.

I happened to again read about Sarah in my personal reading on 23rd April 2016. On that occasion the contributor added, *'God is not mentioned in this passage, and it might sometimes seem that God is absent in times of death and mourning. However, God, in His wisdom has seen* (to it) *that Sarah's death, and Abraham's mourning for her, is included in the canon of Scripture.'* [33] This is a story of deep sorrow, and no doubt, tears, yet it is mingled with a hope beyond death and the grave. I had experienced the sentiments expressed by both Drew and those reading notes on the day I buried my Sandra.

In the final chapter of the Apostle Paul's second letter to Timothy he describes his imminent death as his 'departure', a word used for the loosening of the mooring ropes as a ship begins its journey from the shore. While Paul looked back at his life and service, he was also able to look forward to what lay ahead.

Weeping may endure for a night, but joy cometh in the morning. [34]

---

[32] Genesis 23
[33] Scripture Union Notes – Encounter with God: 23 April 2016
[34] Psalm 30:5b (KJV)

'Her absence is like the sky,
spread over everything.' [35]

CHAPTER 8

Living without Sandra

In many ways this title is a misnomer. 'Existing without Sandra' would be more appropriate.

My perception of the world around me dramatically changed after the events of that dreadful summer of 2014. I had changed and was struggling coming to terms with this. I had lost loved ones: grandparents, aunts, uncles and several close friends.

Just over a year earlier, 2nd April 2013, my highly respected Christian colleague, Stanley Duncan, Chief Executive of the Driver and Vehicle Agency, had tragically died after falling from rocks while fishing at a beauty spot on the North Coast. It was such a shock that Easter Tuesday evening when my manager rang me to break the news. In the briefest of moments I had lost a good friend while the Agency had lost its dedicated leader.

Three months earlier that year (7th January 2013), another confidante, Bert Thompson, an esteemed church elder at Ballyhackamore had died suddenly. Some six weeks after Stanley Duncan's death, Jim Peden's beautiful wife, Jackie, died on 19th May 2013 after her brave 18 months battle with cancer.

Over the years I had spoken at a number of funerals, including that of my grandmother with whom I had been very close since earliest

---

[35] C S Lewis. A Grief Observed

childhood. She lived to the ripe old age of 93. At the other end of the spectrum, there was the funeral of Thomas, a Sunday school pupil, who at 19 years of age was tragically killed in a motorcycle collision near Holywood. I watched his parents weep intensely as I tried to comfort them by reading Psalm 23, pointing out that these were the last verses Thomas had memorised before leaving Sunday school several years earlier. Sandra and I felt deeply for that grieving family.

Speaking at those services served to remind me that death was no respecter of persons when it came to the matter of age. However, with the loss of my Sandra, I was now being challenged by the extent of my ignorance as to its devastating effect. Yes, I had mourned for others, yes, I had a theological understanding of the Bible's teaching about death and the eternal destinies thereafter, and yes, I firmly believed the Scriptures, but I was, nevertheless, unable to accept the reality that *my Sandra* had died. I was ensnared in a tangled web of loss, grief, tears and emptiness.

Having experienced a sustained period of mourning several years earlier, Sandra remarked, "You couldn't live like this, sure you couldn't, Love." I was now beginning to see just how true those words were and how incredibly difficult it is to *live* in a transfixed state of bereavement. The truth is that on each previous occasion grief had always drawn to a close. It may have taken days, weeks or perhaps months, but sure enough, life eventually returned to a state of normality; but not this time. I was unable to fathom such deep grief despite the fact that I had learned a little about the grieving process many years earlier during my time as a Training Officer.

Just after Edward was born in September 1989 I managed to leave the world of Accounts and Financial Planning and enter the much more stimulating [at least for me] world of Management Training. One of the most satisfying courses that I was responsible for delivering during those early 1990s was Team Building. This included giving a brief outline of the 'Change Curve' that was based on a model originally developed in the 1960s by Elisabeth Kubler-

Ross to explain the grieving process.[36] Kubler-Ross proposed that a terminally ill patient would progress through several stages of grief when informed of their illness – *Shock and Denial, Anger and Depression, Acceptance and Integration.*

She further proposed that this model could be applied to any dramatic life-changing situation. Consequently, it has been widely utilised as a method of helping people understand their reactions to significant change or upheaval. The Change Curve was a firm fixture in change management training. I explained the basic tenets and it all seemed so straightforward back then when it was little more than theory. Now I was experiencing its reality.

While accepting that there are common stages in the grieving process I nevertheless became increasingly conscious of the profound personal nature of grief. No one could fully understand how I felt. By the same token I realised that I was unable to comprehend someone else's grief and, therefore, it would be wrong to judge. Having said that, I became frustrated – even angry at times – when someone commented, "You know what it's like Gary" and yet I observed a husband, wife or partner standing close by them.

I think back to that very first Sunday without Sandra. Sunday mornings had always been busy with Sandra frequently preparing dinner for her mum, stepdad, Edward and Anna, but this was not going to happen that day or on any other Sunday ever again. My heart ached at such a thought. Thoughtfully, Anna's parents invited me for dinner that first Sunday. As we shared the meal, it was scarcely believable to think that Sandra had stood up and spoken her farewell words to all of us at that same table exactly two weeks earlier.

Just a few days later, 27th August, heralded what should have been our 28th Wedding Anniversary. That morning I wept as I watched our wedding video and tried to comprehend how our marriage could

---

[36] https://www.exeter.ac.uk/media/universityofexeter/humanresources/documents/learningdevelopment/the_change_curve.pdf

have ended so abruptly. I later went to the cemetery with Edward, and then back to his home in Donaghadee.

As I sat with Edward that afternoon, the telephone rang and he received the welcoming news that a recent interview for a position at Bavarian BMW in Belfast had been successful. How significant it was that he received this confirmation on that day of all days. It was a tiny candle in a very dark place as I thought of how his mum would have been very proud of him embarking on this new phase of his life. Doubtless, if she had been still with us, she would have texted everyone!

The following Sunday, Philip and Rosemary Johnston – friends from Scrabo Hall – kindly invited other family members and me to their home for dinner. I remained deeply subdued while others conversed. I felt the abject loneliness of socialising without Sandra who would contribute so much to any conversation. However, I will always remember the moment following the meal when Rosemary's aged mother (then in her late 90s) broke her silence and calmly asked if she could address me for a few minutes. In the midst of reverential hush she related how she had lost her husband in a car collision, and sometime later, her only son. She comforted me in a way that many others could not because she had walked the path of grief herself. This wise and caring saint is now with the Lord – and with my Sandra.

During those first few months without Sandra I was determined to put the house, and particularly the kitchen, back into some sort of habitable state. It still bore the hallmarks of an unfinished refurbishment. Somehow, I had to complete the job that Sandra and I had started together.

Buying wallpaper was relatively simple since Sandra had already chosen it! But what did I know, much less, care, about tiles, or having the oak kitchen units sprayed. It was most peculiar to see refurbishment work being carried out void of excitement on my part. On the contrary, it brought increasing distress. I had always lived in a *home*—with my parents and sister, and then Sandra and Edward –

but now I was living alone in a *house*. The two experiences were poles apart, and still are. As the saying goes, '*A house is bricks and beams, but a home is love and dreams.*'

Inevitably, financial affairs had to be addressed. I struggled with the notion that Sandra would never reach retirement and enjoy any of the pension entitlements from past employers. Her colleague Susan reassured me that Sandra would have been content knowing I was the recipient.

I also became acutely aware in those early months that should anything happen to me Edward would be left having to sort things out. So, documents I deemed to be no longer of importance were shredded. Everything in the roof space was moved to newly purchased plastic tubs, and duly labelled. Cupboards and drawers were tidied again and again. So many items were also to become redundant: the Christmas tree, decorations, selected kitchen utensils, and a host of other things.

Nevertheless, there was a limit to this de-cluttering and reorganising. For the first time in my life, I began to appreciate my grandmother's unwillingness to change things after my grandfather had died. Her reluctance to discard old furniture, and dispose of clothing and other items, had never made much sense to me. Consequently, many things remained untouched in my house and it almost seemed as if I was expecting Sandra home from work at any moment. (I must confess that after four and a half years virtually all of Sandra's personal belongings remain. Her slippers still sit beside mine and her perfumes, of which she was a connoisseur, still reside in our bedroom wardrobe.)

The few photographs not already in albums were also carefully sorted. I enlarged several of Sandra and positioned them throughout the house so that I would see her face in every room. I found particular comfort in designing a large montage of photographs of us on holiday down through the years. These have become a constant reminder of the beautiful experiences we had shared.

I clung to the precious thoughts of my life with Sandra, although each memory was a double-edged sword since I no longer had my 'co-rememberer'. To quote John Green from *'The Fault in our Stars'* [37] – *'The pleasure of remembering had been taken from me, because there was no longer anyone to remember with. It felt like losing your co-rememberer meant losing the memory itself, as if the things we'd done were less real and important than they had been hours before.'*

Amidst my sorrow and tears were things that brought gratitude and joy. One memory that surpasses all others is of me standing in our bedroom during those last days and simply saying, "Sandra I love you with all my heart," and of her tender reply, "I know you do, Love, I know you do."

I can identify with the sentiments of C S Lewis[38] – *'Grief…gives life a permanently provisional feeling. It doesn't seem worth starting anything. I can't settle down. I yawn, I fidget, I smoke too much. Up till this I always had too little time. Now there is nothing but time. Almost pure time, empty successiveness.'*

I began to walk, or more accurately, stroll, at every opportunity. This got me out of the house and helped alleviate boredom. The nearby Tullynagardy Road, which led out into the countryside, became my 'oasis' although in the darker evenings I opted to walk around Newtownards town centre instead. While walking did not prevent sleeplessness or restlessness during the night hours, it did, perhaps, contribute to the loss of almost two stone in weight during those first six months or so. When I did sleep, I sometimes experienced a recurring dream in which Sandra had not died, but rather, gone missing. Naturally, I wakened disorientated.

Whilst walking, I often thought about all those memorable family holidays, and notably, those spent in the dazzling US Sunshine State

---

[37] https://www.goodreads.com/quotes/485718-the-pleasure-of-remembering-had-been-taken-from-me-because
[38] C S Lewis. A Grief Observed

of Florida. However, I also recalled those gloomy feelings while waiting in the hotel lobby for a bus to come and transport us back to Orlando Airport for our flight home. Sitting there, it no longer mattered if the sun was shining or not, what the pool conditions were like, what tours were available, or what food was to be enjoyed that day. The stark reality was that our marvellous days in the sun were over and you had to face the long tiring flight home. Albeit in a different context, those gloomy feelings now seemed permanent.

Anything remotely enjoyable was 'off limits'. In this new existence, things of personal interest, and indeed passion, were incapable of lifting my spirits. The desire to play football – as I had done for decades – or the occasional round of golf, or game of tennis, was gone. The utter elation I had experienced since childhood when watching West Ham United score a goal was no more. I couldn't remember a time in my life when I had not supported 'the Hammers', and yet, now seeing them win or lose, brought neither joy nor disappointment. I was 'claret and blue through and through' so how could this possibly be?

Life had often resembled a jigsaw puzzle with its countless pieces that always seemed to fit together. But now it was as if the pieces were all over the place. To use another analogy, the 'dots didn't join up' anymore, and in all honesty, there didn't appear to be any more dots left to join up.

Sandra and I usually travelled to and from work together and discussed the events of the day. We attended the church meetings together every Sunday, and again on Tuesday evenings. Wednesday was our 'night in'. In more recent times we had dined out on Thursdays. I had habitually played five-a-side football on Friday nights for decades while Sandra visited her sister. But life was now 'upside down'. For instance, instead of visiting Ards Shopping Centre on Saturday afternoons, I went to Ballyvester Cemetery. I was struck by the contrast; there were no long queues to enter the cemetery, nor ever a problem finding a car parking space.

I dreaded the thought of returning to work. Indeed, I wondered if I could ever find the motivation to go back at all. It seemed so meaningless. I had commenced working as the Driver and Vehicle Agency's Health and Safety Manager in February 2001 and had thoroughly enjoyed the job, but I struggled with the very idea of going back to a post that focussed on trying to maintain *health* and safety in the workplace. It was crazy to think that in some 34 years with the NICS I had probably missed no more than 15 days due to sickness, and now I had been off work for almost six months!

Due to my prolonged absence from work I was asked to attend the NICS Occupational Health Service. After unburdening my heart about Sandra, about us, and about her horrendous battle with cancer, the nurse looked at me and said, "You are one of life's lucky ones." I was shocked! I never believed in the concept of luck, but more to the point, I wondered if she had been listening to what I had said during the previous half an hour or so? Then she kindly explained that in the course of her work she met many folk whose lives had been devastated by marital breakdown, family strife, addictions, debt and other tragic events, and then added, "Many people live a lifetime and never experience the happiness that you and your wife seem to have experienced." The truth of what she was saying then dawned on me and I found peace in a comment that initially brought consternation.

I eventually did return to work on 5th January 2015 and was very appreciative of the personal encouragement of the Chief Executive, Paul Duffy, and my other colleagues. I rather quickly learned to appreciate work, for the primary reason that it served as a distraction from the other things in life that occupied my mind. Perversely, Friday afternoons at 4pm became the worst time of the week as it meant preparing to face another weekend. In the past, and for the purpose of extracting a smile or two, I had joked with colleagues, "Thank goodness it's Monday morning!" but now it had become my sincere new dictum.

Sandra's absence was, indeed, like the sky above; spread over everything.

'Grief never ends...but it changes.
It's a passage, not a place to stay.
Grief is not a sign of weakness, nor a lack of faith...
it is the price of love.' [39]

CHAPTER 9

Learning to Listen in the Loneliness

Living in a house alone in the midst of grief made it very tempting for me to withdraw from the world around me and shut everything out. I was in my own bubble. Participation in family life, church activities, work, and indeed, all aspects of life became a constant struggle. The only person in the world who truly knew me, and with whom I felt totally at ease, was gone. Sandra was able to see right through me as though I were transparent. I could be 'myself' with all my rough edges exposed – and there were many – that only she saw. The assurance of being loved by someone unconditionally, which I took so much for granted, had disappeared. Grief seemed impenetrable and was alleviated, if only briefly, when I left the house for that 'oasis' walk up the nearby Tullynagardy Road.

Thankfully, family and close friends ensured that I didn't get my way all the time as, somewhat reluctantly, I accepted kind invitations for lunch, tea, or perhaps just a chat over coffee. I could talk for hours provided it was about my Sandra. I am indebted to those who took the time to listen, and to those who took time to pray for me, and with me. How true are the words of the Apostle James: *'Religion that*

---

[39] Unknown

God our Father accepts as pure and faultless is this: to look after orphans and widows in their distress...' [40]

Nevertheless, the thought of not 'fitting in' was overwhelming at times. I discovered the extent to which social activities revolved around families and couples, and how that a holiday for one, a table for one, or even a portion of food for one are atypical. I could also sit in a room full of family and friends and still be consumed by loneliness. I could identify with the TV celebrity and journalist, Esther Rantzen, who, after the death of her husband, hit the nail on the head when she said, "Some people define loneliness as having plenty of people to do something with, but nobody to do nothing with." [41] I had 'nobody to do nothing with'.

I have never been the victim of 'identity theft', yet it was as if I had lost my identity. It was odd ticking the 'widower' box on correspondence. There were no letters or invitations arriving in the post for 'Mr and Mrs Carson'. I was no longer one half of 'a couple'. Worst of all, I was no longer *My Gary*. Thankfully, I was still a father.

How was I going to carry on? How was I going to adapt? Where could I get help? Did I even want help? Would my faith in God survive? Should I accept prescription drugs that would numb my senses a little and make me feel a bit more upbeat? Very little was making sense as these endless questions flooded my mind.

Doctors had briefly mentioned medication during one of my initial visits to obtain a medical certificate, but I never gave that option any serious thought. I had no desire to be lulled into some kind of happier consciousness. I also turned down offers of counselling, although, in hindsight, this may have helped.

Slowly, very slowly, I began to listen in the loneliness; particularly to others who had been bereaved, and ultimately, God Himself.

---

[40] James 1:27 (NIV)
[41] https://www.yours.co.uk/features/celebrity/articles/esther-rantzen-speaks-out

The countless sympathy cards that I had received in the wake of Sandra's death touched me deeply. I left two sitting conspicuously in the living room month after month. One came from Aileen, a school friend of Sandra's, whose own mother had died tragically at a very young age. I could almost hear Sandra's voice as I read the verses and tried to accept the last verse in particular –

> *If I should go before you do,*
> *Live the life still ahead of you.*
> *Why should life stop because I am gone?*
> *Life is for living, and you must carry on.*
> *Strengthen yourself, my precious one.*
> *We'll meet again, one blessed morn.*

The other card came from Shirl, a colleague from work. Her beloved husband died suddenly not long after she had sent me the card. I found real comfort in her poignant handwritten quotation: *'Grief never ends... but it changes. It's a passage, not a place to stay. Grief is not a sign of weakness, nor a lack of faith... it is the price of love.'*

Geraldine, another ex colleague sent a very memorable e-mail that drew my attention to a thought provoking article that apparently went 'viral' across the Internet several years earlier.[42] The lengthy text, challenging, yet encouraging, read –

Someone on reddit wrote the following heartfelt plea online: 'My friend just died. I don't know what to do.' A lot of people responded. Then there's one older guy's incredible comment that stood out from the rest that might just change the way we approach life and death:

'Alright, here goes. I'm old. What that means is that I've survived (so far) and a lot of people I've known and loved did not. I've lost friends, best friends, acquaintances, co-workers, grandparents, relatives, teachers, mentors, students, neighbours, and a host of other

---

[42] http://abellfuneralhome.com/blogs/blog-entries/5/Waves-of-Grief/4/Waves-of-Grief.html#blog-start

folks. I have no children, and I can't imagine the pain it must be to lose a child. But here's my two cents.

I wish I could say you get used to people dying. I never did. I don't want to. It tears a hole through me whenever somebody I love dies, no matter the circumstances. But I don't want it to "not matter." I don't want it to be something that just passes. My scars are a testament to the love and the relationship that I had for and with that person. And if the scar is deep, so was the love. So be it. Scars are a testament to life. Scars are a testament that I can love deeply and live deeply and be cut, or even gouged, and that I can heal and continue to live and continue to love. And the scar tissue is stronger than the original flesh ever was. Scars are a testament to life. Scars are only ugly to people who can't see.

As for grief, you'll find it comes in waves. When the ship is first wrecked, you're drowning, with wreckage all around you. Everything floating around you reminds you of the beauty and the magnificence of the ship that was, and is no more. And all you can do is float. You find some piece of the wreckage and you hang on for a while. Maybe it's some physical thing. Maybe it's a happy memory or a photograph. Maybe it's a person who is also floating. For a while, all you can do is float. Stay alive.

In the beginning, the waves are 100 feet tall and crash over you without mercy. They come 10 seconds apart and don't even give you time to catch your breath. All you can do is hang on and float. After a while, maybe weeks, maybe months, you'll find the waves are still 100 feet tall, but they come further apart. When they come, they still crash all over you and wipe you out. But in between, you can breathe, you can function. You never know what's going to trigger the grief. It might be a song, a picture, a street intersection, the smell of a cup of coffee. It can be just about anything...and the wave comes crashing. But in between waves, there is life.

Somewhere down the line, and it's different for everybody, you find that the waves are only 80 feet tall. Or 50 feet tall. And while they still come, they come further apart. You can see them coming. An anniversary, a birthday, or Christmas, or landing at O'Hare. You can see it coming, for the most part, and prepare yourself. And when it washes over you, you know that somehow you will, again, come out on the other side. Soaking wet, sputtering, still hanging on to some tiny piece of the wreckage, but you'll come out.

Take it from an old guy. The waves never stop coming, and somehow you don't really want them to. But you learn that you'll survive them. And other waves will come. And you'll survive them too. If you're lucky, you'll have lots of scars from lots of loves. And lots of shipwrecks.'

Sandra and I often joked about enjoying 'ordinary' days during the year just as much as the 'special' days that we or society has designated. Now each designated day became a 'northeaster' – the 3rd November, with all that it meant to both of us, our birthdays, Edward's birthday, Mothers Day, Fathers Day, St Valentine's Day, Christmas Day, and to me, the day with the most fearsome 'winds' of all, New Year's Eve. A new 'special day' – the 20th of each month – also came into my life. Sandra had been taken into hospital on the 20th of July and died on the 20th of August. On each '20th' I have found comfort by taking leave and going to the cemetery with a posse of flowers prepared meticulously by the local florist, Petal Power.

I have learned to brace myself as I see each of these inescapable storms approaching. Sometimes, though, I have also knowingly ventured into other storms by visiting a church, a restaurant or some other place that Sandra and I went to together, or perhaps, by playing a piece of music or looking through one of our holiday albums.

It is much more difficult, though, trying to 'stay afloat' when a storm strikes unexpectedly. For example, that moment when sitting with another couple in a restaurant and the waitress asked if there was still one more person to come; that moment when a Payment Protection Insurance (PPI) agent telephoned and asked if Sandy Carson is available as he has some good news for her; that moment when I purchased more flowers at a garage and the cashier asked if I'm trying to put someone in a good mood that day; that moment when I heard a newsreader's voice on the radio and recalled the fact that Sandra had booked their honeymoon.

What then of my personal faith in God, and in His Son, Jesus Christ? He is the one who '...*arose, and rebuked the wind, and said unto the sea, "Peace, be still". And the wind ceased, and there was a great calm.'* [43]

During the initial weeks and months without Sandra, many fellow believers tried to comfort me by texting a verse of Scripture or the lines of a hymn. At that stage in the grieving process, however, I was numb and unable to even begin to digest what had happened. It might seem a strange thing for a Christian to say, but most of those well-intentioned messages meant little to me. In the words of a popular song from the 1980s, I felt as though I had experienced a *'Total Eclipse of the Heart'.*[44]

> *Once upon a time there was light in my life,*
> *But now there's only love in the dark,*
> *Nothing I can say,*
> *A total eclipse of the heart.*

Thankfully though, one or two verses were like faint lights penetrating the thick fog. For instance, I recall a friend, Darren, gently reminding me of how the Lord Jesus was actually standing right beside Mary while she wept at the garden tomb after His resurrection. Mary had faithfully followed the Lord and knew Him well, but her heart was now broken, and in the darkness of the early morning, she initially didn't recognise him.[45]

During my speech at Edward and Anna's wedding, I quoted the final words of the Lord Jesus in Matthew's Gospel ere he left His disciples,

---

[43] Mark 4:39 (KJV)
[44] https://www.azlyrics.com/lyrics/bonnietyler/totaleclipseoftheheart.html
[45] John 20:11-18

to return to Heaven: '*I am with you alway...*' [46] That promise had always meant a great deal to me. In fact, the text hung on the wall of our home throughout married life. On that blissful day back in June 2013 I referred to the fact that the word *alway* simply meant 'all the days' and reassured Edward and Anna that the Lord would be with them during the good days and the bad days that would surely come. Somehow, I now had to *listen* again to that promise.

Despite everything that had happened, I still retained the desire to attend church meetings on Sundays. However, I couldn't contemplate the thought of returning to the little fellowship at Ballyhackamore and to the range of activities I had been so heavily involved in for a lifetime. While I had such deep affection for those who met there, and still visit occasionally, I knew that a permanent return was going to be a bridge too far so to speak. In fact, I had told Sandra during her illness that I couldn't go back without her and that I would, instead, go to Scrabo Hall with Edward and Anna. Therefore, within a matter of weeks I started attending Scrabo, albeit strictly as a visitor. (Sadly, if perhaps understandably, it was almost three years before I finally wrote a letter of resignation to the folk at Ballyhackamore. At the same time I requested membership at Scrabo.)

Nevertheless, participation in meetings was out of the question. In fact, even something as rudimentary as singing in church became a terrible strain. For a period of 18 months or so I sat in silence and almost stubbornly refused to sing. I consoled myself by thinking of the words in one of the despondent Psalms.

> *By the rivers of Babylon we sat and wept, when we remembered Zion. There on the poplars we hung our harps. For there our captors asked us for songs, our tormentors demanded songs of joy; they said, "Sing us one of the songs of Zion!" "How can we sing the songs of the LORD's while in a foreign land."* [47]

---

[46] Matthew 28:10 (KJV)
[47] Psalm 137:1-4 (NIV)

The author of that Psalm had struggled with the pain of remembering tragedy and loss. The Judean exile of 587 BC had caused great anguish for the whole nation and the exiled people of Israel found it difficult to sing in the strange land of Babylon that was so very far from Jerusalem and home. In like manner, I found it hard to sing in this strange land of unrelenting grief where I felt captive.

Indeed, I began to question the language and sentiments expressed in some of the hymns and songs. A popular modern song referred to God as 'My lighthouse, shining in the darkness'. I had no issue with this truth, but rather, with its relevance to me as I reasoned that the ship 'MV Gary & Sandra' had been struck by the deadly missile of pancreatic cancer and had sunk leaving nothing but wreckage. In another song there is a prayer for God to 'Reign in me, over all my dreams, in my darkest hour'. I couldn't grasp the link as I reckoned that the darkest hour was bereft of dreams. I recalled days in the past when I had enthusiastically sung, 'All of my ambitions, hopes and plans I surrender these into your hands.' I felt naked without ambitions, hopes or plans. I held to the truths but struggled with the personal application.

However, I continued to listen as Christian friends opened their hearts to express their own feelings after the loss of a loved one. I recall shaking the hand of a speaker when leaving Scrabo Hall one Sunday evening several months after Sandra's death. I greatly respected his father, who not only presented the Christian message with such wisdom and clarity, but whose life had mirrored that teaching. (I was very touched when the speaker participated in his funeral a number of years earlier.) During the handshake he related how that after his mother died, his father said, "It's like falling down a pit and thinking you have reached the bottom and then realising that you are only on a ledge. You fall a little further and think surely this must be the bottom – but no, just another ledge and so on, and on it goes." Such raw honesty was extremely reassuring.

I listened to Eleanor, another Christian friend who had been widowed while pregnant in her early 20's, and who visited me at home with

Finbar, her second husband, very shortly after Sandra's death. After relaying how she felt in her own dark days many years earlier, she said, "Gary there is one thing that will help you as time passes; Sandra was yours." Oh, what a precious thought to cling to.

Some friends gave me books about bereavement, but I had never been an avid reader. Sandra could have lifted a book and be totally engrossed in it until it was finished, but not me. Yes, I had often sat in my little study surrounded by Bible commentaries while preparing a message, but rarely did I read a book cover to cover. The writings of the Christian apologist C S Lewis were something of an exception though. Born in Belfast, he held academic positions in both Oxford and Cambridge Universities and boldly declared, *'I believe in Christianity as I believe that the sun has risen: not only because I see it, but because by it I see everything else.'* [48] I found his books *Mere Christianity, The Screwtape Letters* and the legendary *The Lion, the Witch and the Wardrobe* to be among the most influential that I had read.

C S Lewis also lost his wife to cancer. He later wrote the book *A Grief Observed.* I found it comforting to know that a Christian of his calibre, who struggled so intensively with the death of his wife, was able to admit, *'The death of a beloved is an amputation.'* He added, *'Talk to me about the truth of religion and I'll listen gladly. Talk to me about the duty of religion and I'll listen submissively. But don't come talking to me about the consolations of religion or I shall suspect that you don't understand.'* [49]

Those words provided much succour to me when people would offer 'consolations' such as: *'Sandra wouldn't want to be back here you know'; 'You will see her again'* or *'She is just a little bit ahead of you'.* Again, it is not that these statements are untrue, and how very thankful I am for that, but when I hear them, I suspect, as C S Lewis did, that the other person simply does not understand, nor indeed will, until they go through that experience themselves.

---

[48] https://www.brainyquote.com/quotes/c_s_lewis_162523
[49] C S Lewis. A Grief Observed

My own personal daily Bible readings helped to keep me afloat as I tried to *listen to God* through His word. The Scripture Union's (SU) *Encounter with God* booklet habitually includes the reading of a Psalm each Sunday, and looking back I note that on Sunday, 24th August, the day after Sandra was buried, I read the following verses – [50]

> *If the LORD had not been on our side – let Israel say – "if the LORD had not been on our side when people attacked us, they would have swallowed us alive when their anger flared against us; the flood would have engulfed us, the torrent would have swept over us, the raging waters would have swept us away." Praise be to the LORD, who has not let us be torn by their teeth. We have escaped like a bird from the fowler's snare; the snare has been broken, and we have escaped. Our help is in the name of the LORD, the Maker of heaven and earth.*

It appears that these verses brought support during those dreadful days as I noted how I had inserted several exclamation marks beside the contributor's comment: *'Though everything changes about us, our great God cannot be changed.'*

The Psalms are full of life's events and God's response, and essentially fall into two categories; those that focus on thanksgiving and praise to God, and those described as Laments i.e. complaints relating to human experiences and how they make us feel. In the latter of these, we discover that it is OK for believers to express negative feelings to God. It is OK for believers to complain bitterly about what is happening to them. God can cope with any question we might raise, and He has no difficulty with our asking. I thank God for the sheer openness of these Psalms, and for the fact that they include situations of extreme crisis when, from the objective point of view, all seems lost. Yet, each lament is not without hope as we see how the Lord lives and brings deliverance to those who trust in Him.

---

[50] Psalm 124:1-8 (NIV)

I found comfort in Psalm 142, the heading of which states that it was a prayer when David was in the cave. There, he speaks of loneliness and tells God of his trouble and how his spirit was overwhelmed within him. Two possible situations have been suggested for this, with both occurring when King Saul was in pursuit of David.[51] I think of the awful darkness inside that cave. In spite of his confidence that God watched over his way he still voiced his complaint, appealing to God to hear him. That confidence did not change his current situation, which was one of desperation. He was downcast, but cried to the Lord for help with the hope that one day he would be able to praise the Lord again.

The Bible is not afraid to record the weeping and mourning that accompanies death. I think of David's haunting lamentation for Saul and Jonathan[52] and for his son Absalom[53], and the grief of Mary and Martha after the death of their brother, Lazarus.[54] I think also of Matthew's Gospel and how he records the callous murder of John the Baptist before telling us that *'his disciples came and took up the body, and buried it, and went and told Jesus.'* [55] How precious it is to think that in hours of heartbreaking bereavement the best thing to do is to go and tell Jesus.

On 18th July 2014 – just three days before Sandra was diagnosed – the Christian writer Jon Bloom published the article titled, *When God Seems Silent.* [56] This was brought to my attention through the SU reading notes some three and a half years later (7th January 2018) when meditating on Psalm 77. Here is an extract from his article –

> *God can be maddeningly hard to get. When God says that his ways are not our ways, he really means it (Isaiah 55:8).*

---

[51] 1 Samuel 22:1 and 24:3
[52] 1 Samuel 1
[53] 2 Samuel 18
[54] John 11
[55] Matthew 14:12 (AV)
[56] "When God Seems Silent" https://www.desiringgod.org/articles/when-god-seems-silent

We have these encounters with him where he breaks into our lives with power and answers our prayers and wins our trust and waters the garden of our faith, making it lush and green.

And then there are these seasons when chaos careens with apparent carelessness through our lives and the world, leaving us shattered. Or an unrelenting darkness descends. Or an arid wind we don't even understand blows across our spiritual landscape, leaving the crust of our soul cracked and parched. And we cry to God in our confused anguish and he just seems silent. He seems absent.

Atheists will tell us that the reason God seems silent is because *he's absent. "No one's home at that address. Duh."*

In the silent suffering seasons we can be tempted to believe it. Until we step back and take a look and see that existence itself is not silent. It screams God (Romans 1:20). As Parmenides said, and as Maria sang in The Sound of Music, "Nothing comes from nothing; nothing ever could."

Believing atheism is like moderns believing in a flat earth. "From where I stand, it doesn't look like God is there." Right. And if you only trust your perceptions, the world looks flat. The only reason you know the world is round is because of authoritative scientific revelation and many corroborating testimonies.

What we experience as God's absence or distance or silence is phenomenological. It's how we perceive it. It's how at some point it looks and feels but it isn't how it is. Just like we can experience the world as flat when we're walking on a huge spinning ball, we can experience God as absent or distant when 'in him we live and move and have our being' (Acts 17:28).

...So you desire God and ask for more of him and what do you get? Stuck in a desert feeling deserted. You feel disoriented and desperate. Don't despair. The silence, the absence is phenomenological. It's how

it feels, it's not how it is. You are not alone. God is with you (Psalm 23:4). And he is speaking all the time in the priceless gift of his objective word so you don't need to rely on the subjective impressions of your fluctuating emotions..."

I conclude this chapter by referring to what is arguably the best known Psalm and passage in the Old Testament Scriptures, Psalm 23. Here is a brief but beautiful account of 'a day in the life of a sheep'. The renowned US actor James Stewart tells of how his stepson had been killed in action during the Vietnam war and how, in his distress, he found comfort in the following inspirational and reassuring poem, *He Leadeth Me*, written by Rev. John F. Chaplain, and based on this Psalm.[57] It has often sustained me too.

'In pastures green?' - Not always. Sometimes
He, who knoweth best, in kindness leadeth me
In weary ways, where heavy shadows be;
Out of the sunshine warm and soft and bright,
Out of the sunshine into darkest night;
I oft would faint with sorrow and affright,
Only for this, I know He holds my hand;
So whether led in green or desert land,
I trust, although I may not understand.

'And by still waters?' - No, not always so.
Oft times the heavy tempests round me blow,
And o'er my soul the waves and billows go.
But when the storm beats loudest, and I cry
Aloud for help, the Master standeth by,
And whispers to my soul, 'Lo, it is I!'
Above the tempest wild I hear Him say,
'Beyond the darkness lies the perfect day;
In every path of thine I lead the way'.

---

[57] http://golden-nuggets-flbc.blogspot.co.uk/2012/11/poem-by-rev-john-f-chaplain-he-leadeth.html

So, whether on the hilltops high and fair
I dwell, or in the sunless valleys where
The shadows lie, what matter? He is there;
And more than this, where'er the pathway
Lead He gives to me no helpless broken reed,
But His own hand, sufficient for my need.
So where He leads me I can safely go;
And in the blest hereafter I shall know
Why, in His wisdom, He hath led me so.

CHAPTER 10

Pancreatic Cancer –
a 'silent cancer'

This chapter relies heavily on information obtained from various websites. Some of the detail, be it statistics or otherwise, can be an amalgam from any of the following three charities; the Pancreatic Cancer Research Fund, Pancreatic Cancer Action and Pancreatic Cancer UK, as cited in the footnotes.

Cancer Research UK recently estimated that one in two of those born in the UK after 1960 would be diagnosed with some form of cancer during their lifetime.[59] One in two is such a frightening statistic.

Having been a Health and Safety practitioner in some guise or other for the most part of my career, I am acutely aware of the danger of carcinogenic substances [capable of causing cancer] within the workplace, and of the need to ensure that employees are adequately protected. The Institution of Occupational Safety and Health (IOSH) has drawn attention to the overall impact cancer is having upon society and points out that around 330,000 adults in the UK are diagnosed with cancer every year. The Institution does, however, acknowledge that half of those diagnosed currently survive at least

---

[58] https://www.worldwidecancerresearch.org/blog-post/latest-stats-show-60-people-know-almost-nothing-disease/
[59] http://www.cancerresearchuk.org/health-professional/cancer-statistics/risk/lifetime-risk

ten years and that many – up to 84% of those working when they receive their diagnosis – return to work.[60]

Such figures offer hope by highlighting the fact that a cancer diagnosis does not have to be a death sentence. Many who suffer the disease can be given treatment that will enable them to live a substantially normal life, if not recover fully. Sadly, pancreatic cancer is very different; at least for the overwhelming majority of those diagnosed.

I had absolutely no understanding of pancreatic cancer prior to 2014, much less the controversial 'I wish I had' advertising campaign run by the charity Pancreatic Cancer Action (PCA) in February of that year.[61] The objective of that campaign was to raise awareness of this particular cancer and its symptoms. It featured three patients aged 42, 24, and 51, with each, respectively, expressing a wish that they had been diagnosed with testicular, breast and cervical cancer. Devastating and all as that would be, it would at least have offered them a 97%, 85% and 67% chance of survival.

Pancreatic cancer, which affects men and women equally, is undeniably the deadliest disease of its kind. The following statistics provided by the PCA are startling and generally depressing – [62]

- *Pancreatic cancer is the 5th biggest cancer killer in the UK*
- *It is the UK's 11th most common cancer*
- *27 people are newly diagnosed each day (9,921 people in 2015)*
- *24 people will die each day (8,912 people in 2015)*
- *5-year survival is less than 7%. This figure has not improved significantly in almost 50 years and is the worst survival rate of the 22 most common cancers*
- *Relative survival to one year is less than 20% with the UK having one of the worst rates in Europe*

---

[60] IOSH Publication: 2 Feb 2017.
[61] https://pancreaticcanceraction.org/about/what-we-do/symptoms-aware-ness/advertising-campaigns/campaign/
[62] https://pancreaticcanceraction.org/about-pancreatic-cancer/medical-professionals/stats-facts/facts-and-statistics/

- *Patients able to have surgery to remove the tumour have up to a 30% chance of surviving 5 years*
- *Only 10% of patients are eligible for potentially curative surgery due to late diagnosis*

(While cited by PCA in 2018 these figures relate to 2015 because the reporting system for cancer statistics varies with the cancer registries across the countries of the United Kingdom and for mortality published by the ONS, there is usually a delay of approximately 18 months for the collation of incidence and of 12 months for the collation of mortality figures.)

It is predicted that by the year 2026, 11,279 people will die every year from the disease in Britain alone. This is a 28% increase on 2014 when the disease was responsible for taking the life of my beloved Sandra. It will make pancreatic cancer the fourth biggest killer after lung, bowel and prostate cancers, according to the charity Pancreatic Cancer UK.[63]

How does Northern Ireland fare specifically? PCA has confirmed that in 2015 the disease was 41% more common than in 2010. This is significantly higher than the UK average, which has seen rates rise by 17% in the same five-year period. A total of 273 people were diagnosed with pancreatic cancer in 2015, and because of the low survival rate of just 5%, only 14 of them are likely to survive until 2020.[64] But Northern Ireland, and indeed the UK as a whole, is far from unique as in nearly every country pancreatic cancer is the only major cancer with a single digit five-year survival rate (2-9%).[65]

The statistics are dire, mainly because of the lack of a medical breakthrough, and yet pancreatic cancer remains chronically underfunded compared with many other cancers. It receives just over 3% of overall cancer research funding: a total of only £14 million in

---

[63] http://www.dailymail.co.uk/health/article-4224052/Pancreatic-cancer-set-cancer-killers.html
[64] https://www.belfasttelegraph.co.uk/news/call-for-more-action-on-pan-creatic-cancer-as-rates-of-disease-in-ni-continue-to-climb-36561966.html
[65] https://www.cancer.org/content/dam/cancer-org/research/cancer-facts-and-statistics/global-cancer-facts-and-figures/global-cancer-facts-and-figures-2nd-edition.pdf

2016/17[66] The pancreatic cancer charities across the UK are determined to lead a revolution for people affected by funding research to allow more patients to be diagnosed much earlier as, sadly, most are diagnosed too late to receive life-saving surgery.

PCA points out that nearly 50% of cases are diagnosed as an emergency after patients have arrived at hospital via A&E, as happened in Sandra's case. With the average life expectancy on diagnosis being 2 to 6 months,[67] Sandra's passing after just four weeks was unusually short. The Government needs to play its part in prioritizing research since pancreatic cancer cannot be allowed to languish in the 'too-hard-to-deal-with' category.

On World Pancreatic Cancer Day, 17th November 2016, attention was drawn to the alarming statistic arising from a worldwide survey that 60% of people know 'almost nothing' about pancreatic cancer! [68] The challenge, therefore, is to elevate the global conversation in the hope that much more will be done to combat this horrific disease. I trust that this book and this chapter in particular, will go some way in support of that objective.

To help us have a better understanding of pancreatic cancer it is important to consider the purpose of the pancreas, the causes and symptoms of the disease, the diagnosis 'stages', and the treatment options available.

What is the pancreas?

The pancreas gland, often described as having a head, body and tail, lies behind the stomach and in front of the spine. Several large and important organs and blood vessels surround it. In very plain terms, it works to help the body use and store energy from food by producing hormones to control blood sugar levels and digestive enzymes to break down food.

---

[66] https://pancreaticcanceraction.org/about-pancreatic-cancer/medical-professionals/stats-facts/facts-and-statistics/
[67] https://pancreaticcanceraction.org/about-pancreatic-cancer/medical-professionals/stats-facts/facts-and-statistics/
[68] https://www.worldwidecancerresearch.org/blog-post/latest-stats-show-60-people-know-almost-nothing-disease/

Causes and symptoms of pancreatic cancer

Pancreatic cancer occurs when abnormal cells in the pancreas grow out of control, forming a mass of tissue called a tumour. As previously mentioned, pancreatic cancers are divided into two main groups: Exocrine tumours and Endocrine tumours, with the former being by far the more common.

The cause of most pancreatic cancers is still unknown. For the few recognised risk factors (e.g., familial history, smoking, obesity, age), more research is required to understand their direct relationship to the disease. While patients diagnosed in time for surgery have a much higher likelihood of surviving five years and beyond early detection remains so very difficult as symptoms can frequently be vague in the initial stages. These can include indigestion, abdominal or mid back pain, unexplained weight loss, jaundice and itching, loss of appetite, pain on eating, nausea and vomiting, changes in stools and new onset diabetes.

Many symptoms are often subtle and can be attributed to less serious, albeit more common, conditions. Indeed, Sandra had most of the abovementioned symptoms, however, and it was suggested that she could have been suffering from gallstones, gastritis or maybe even a hernia. Unfortunately, this was not the case. All this proves how vital it is to make an appointment with a GP as soon as possible after any of the symptoms show up. With many not appearing until the cancer has already reached an advanced stage it is understandable why pancreatic cancer is sometimes referred to as a 'silent cancer'. [69]

Diagnosis

Medical consultants are very much dependent upon being able to get swift access to the necessary scanning equipment, such as CT, in order to provide an accurate diagnosis. Test results will usually be explained in terms of 'staging', which describes the size of a cancer and how far it has spread. This, in turn, will generally dictate the form of treatment.

---

[69] http://www.pcrf.org.uk/pages/about-pancreatic-cancer.html

- *Stage 1*

The earliest stage – the cancer is contained inside the pancreas. This is known as early, localised or resectable pancreatic cancer. It may be possible to operate to remove the cancer (resectable).

- *Stage 2*

The cancer has started to grow into the duodenum, bile duct or tissues around the pancreas, or there may be cancer in the lymph nodes near the pancreas. Lymph nodes are small glands found around the body, which are part of the immune system. This may be resectable pancreatic cancer and it may be possible to operate to remove the cancer, depending on how far the cancer has grown.

- *Stage 3*

The cancer has spread into the stomach, spleen, and large bowel or into large blood vessels near the pancreas. This is usually locally advanced or unresectable pancreatic cancer, meaning it is not possible to remove the cancer with surgery (unresectable). However, it may very occasionally be borderline resectable cancer meaning that it may be possible to remove the cancer, but this will depend upon which blood vessels are affected.

- *Stage 4*

The cancer has spread to other parts of the body such as the lungs or liver. This is known as advanced or metastatic pancreatic cancer. It's not possible to remove the cancer with surgery (unresectable), as surgery can't remove all the cancer cells once they have spread to other parts of the body.

The team of medical professionals responsible for treatment and care is referred to as the 'multidisciplinary team' (MDT). Health professionals are most likely to include a specialist nurse, gastroenterologist, oncologist, surgeon and dietician. Treatment options will depend on whether it is possible to remove the cancer with surgery. But even if surgery isn't possible chemotherapy may be used to slow down the growth of the cancer while there are treatments to help with symptoms.

When surgery to remove the cancer is possible

- *Surgery*

Surgery to completely remove the cancer is possible if the cancer is small, there are no signs that it has spread beyond the pancreas (especially to the large blood vessels nearby) and the patient is fit and healthy. This is known as resectable (operable) cancer. Surgery is the most effective treatment for early stage pancreatic cancer. Unfortunately only one or two out of ten patients can have surgery, as it is very hard to diagnose at the early stage.

Some tumours may be very close to the major blood vessels near the pancreas. These may be called borderline resectable tumours. This means that it may be possible to remove the tumour, but it depends which blood vessels are affected and how far the cancer has grown. Occasionally chemotherapy, and sometimes radiotherapy, may be offered before surgery to try to shrink the cancer and make surgery more successful. Sadly surgeons can find that once they have started an operation it isn't actually possible to remove the cancer.

There are several different operations and these involve removing all or part of the pancreas and sometimes other structures around it. The *Whipple's operation* (pancreaticoduodenectomy) is the most common type of surgery.

- *Chemotherapy*

Chemotherapy uses anti-cancer drugs to destroy cancer cells. It may be given after surgery to remove the cancer, to try to reduce the chances of the cancer coming back. It may also occasionally be offered before surgery.

- *Radiotherapy*

Radiotherapy uses high-energy x-rays (radiation) to destroy cancer cells. Occasionally it is offered before surgery to shrink the cancer or it may be offered after surgery, to try to make sure no cancer cells are left. Radiotherapy may be given together with chemotherapy (chemoradiotherapy).

When surgery to remove the cancer isn't possible
Other treatments can help to control the growth of the cancer, relieve any symptoms it is causing and generally improve how someone is feeling.

● *Treatment to relieve a blocked duodenum or bile duct*
If the cancer blocks the duodenum food isn't able to get through to the bowel and therefore builds up in the stomach causing discomfort, sickness and vomiting. If the bile duct is blocked it can cause jaundice with its symptoms including yellow skin and eyes, and itching. In both situations a small plastic or metal tube (stent) can be inserted and should open up the duodenum or bile duct. Sandra benefited from this latter procedure.

● *Chemotherapy*
If someone has locally advanced pancreatic cancer, chemotherapy or chemotherapy combined with radiotherapy (chemoradiotherapy) can be used to shrink the cancer, slow down its growth, and relieve symptoms. For some people, this treatment shrinks the cancer enough to make surgery possible.

In the case of advanced pancreatic cancer, chemotherapy can be used to slow down the growth of the cancer and relieve symptoms. It won't cure the cancer, but it may enable people to live longer and improve the quality of daily life.

● *Radiotherapy*
Radiotherapy may be an option in the case of locally advanced pancreatic cancer. It is most commonly used together with chemotherapy (chemoradiotherapy).

Radiotherapy or chemoradiotherapy won't cure the cancer, but may help control it and slow down its growth. In a small number of cases, treatment can shrink inoperable tumours enough to make it possible to remove them with surgery.

Radiotherapy can also be helpful in cases of advanced pancreatic cancer. The aim is to control and relieve symptoms, and improve the quality of daily life. Radiotherapy used in this way is called palliative radiotherapy.

Family portrait during Edward's final year at school – 2005/06

Edward with Anna at his 21st birthday party on 14th September 2010

In Glasgow on our 25th wedding anniversary on 27th August 2011

Edward and Anna's engagement on 26th June 2012

Edward's graduation on 4th July 2012

Edward and Anna's wedding on 26th June 2013

A very proud mum and dad!

Sandra with her life long friends Evelyn and Audrey

Sandra with Brooke who said,
"I will miss her hugs"

Sandra with her friend Anne at the wedding of Anne's daughter, Louise, in Glasgow on 10th July 2013

Sandra with Anne's grand-daughter, Isabelle, who has fought her own battle with cancer

Sandra with her friend Pamela during our Mediterranean cruise in September – October 2013

Sandra viewing the city of Lisbon, Portugal, during the Mediterranean cruise

*'Portrait time' aboard The Eclipse during the Mediterranean cruise in September –
October 2013*

Edward and Anna, Sandra's 'two precious people', at our home on Christmas Day 2013 – our last Christmas together as a family

Sandra with Anna at a wedding on 28th December 2013

At the wedding of Heather and Trevor's daughter, Rachel, on 10th June 2014

The last photograph taken of Sandra on 28th July 2014 - one week after her diagnosis and just three weeks before she died

A play swing erected in 'Sandy's' memory by Delia Aston, Clubworld Travel, in Oradea, northwest Romania. A team of volunteers from the Northern Ireland travel trade had travelled there to build homes in association with Habitat for Humanity.

Psalm 57:1 (NIV). 'Have mercy on me, my God, have mercy on me, for in you I take refuge. I will take refuge in the shadow of your wings until the disaster has passed.'

My Sandra

Truly blessed

Pancreatic cancer is much more than statistics and medical terms — it's about people

At the end of the day though pancreatic cancer is not about shocking statistics or complex medical terminology it is about real people whose lives have been devastated by this horrible disease.

I knew that Sandra would have preferred donations to a cancer charity in lieu of flowers. Consequently, this was reflected in the death notice in the Belfast Telegraph. As it happened, the donations were forwarded to the Pancreatic Cancer Research Fund instead of another charity that had been designated. I am so thankful for that little 'error', as it was responsible for bringing me into contact with a Northern Ireland Pancreatic Cancer Support Group that held monthly meetings at the Mater Hospital in Belfast.

This afforded me the opportunity to meet monthly with folks like Brian, Susan, Kerry, Lynn, Liz and others, who's loved ones also died early in life due to the disease. Time after time I heard these people speak of their loved one feeling unwell, and after having visited their GP, being given assurances that there was probably nothing much to worry about. Then, suddenly, they were given the dreadful news that their loved one was terminally ill, and had died within weeks or, at best, months. I also listened to one or two like Ivan, who, because of an early diagnosis, survived and have become an inspiration to others. These group members, hitherto strangers, bonded together because of their common experiences of pancreatic cancer. We spoke the 'same language' and therein, found comfort.

As with certain other diseases, pancreatic cancer is no respecter of persons or age. In recent years the disease has led to the death of a number of celebrities who, despite their fame or wealth, were unable to defeat it. Here are some notable examples –

Luciano Pavarotti, the first ever classical musician to reach the top of the UK pop charts with his performance of *Nessun Dorma* during the 1990 World Cup, and hailed as one of the greatest tenors of all time, was diagnosed in July 2006. He lived for just over a year before succumbing to its deadly consequences in September 2007 at the age of 71.

The actor Patrick Swayze died on 14th September 2009 at the age of 57. He confessed that he started to notice something was wrong on New Year's Eve, 2007, when he couldn't drink a glass of champagne. He soon realised that his indigestion issues were constant and that he was suffering from jaundice and was rapidly losing weight. After a battery of tests, doctors discovered that he had Stage 4 pancreatic cancer. As indicated earlier, removal by surgery at that advanced stage was not an option. While the majority of such patients die within six months of diagnosis, Swayze bravely fought it for 20 months. He said, "I keep dreaming of a future, a future with a long and healthy life, not lived in the shadow of cancer but in the light." [70]

Steve Jobs, co-founder of the computer giant Apple, was another high-profile victim of the disease. A technical innovator and visionary credited with 'Changing the world', fell victim to the more rare form of the cancer – a neuroendocrine tumour – in October 2011 and died at the age of 56. This was seven years after his initial diagnosis. Surgeons had successfully performed the *Whipple's procedure* in July 2004 and then, later, a liver transplant in April 2009 which allowed him to return to work for a period. In early 2011 Jobs witnessed the launch of the iPad 2 and the introduction of the iCloud, but with a deterioration of health, he resigned as Chief Executive of Apple in August of that year before dying a few months later. When diagnosed, he, too, acknowledged that he didn't know what a pancreas was!

During an address to students at Stanford University in the United States in 2005 Steve Jobs stated –

When I was 17, I read a quote that went something like: 'If you live each day as if it was your last, someday you'll most certainly be right.' It made an impression on me, and since then, for the past 33 years, I have looked in the mirror every morning and asked myself: 'If today

---

[70] http://news.bbc.co.uk/1/hi/entertainment/7815115.stm

were the last day of my life, would I want to do what I am about to do today?' And whenever the answer has been 'No' for too many days in a row, I know I need to change something. Remembering that I'll be dead soon is the most important tool that I've ever encountered to help me make the big choices in life. Because almost everything, all external expectations, all pride, all fear of embarrassment or failure – these things just fall away in the face of death, leaving only what is truly important.[71]

Many folk tell me that 'time is a great healer'. Personally, I do not see it that way. Rather, it is a constant reminder that life is short, as Jobs and others discovered. In an odd way, this brings solace. It's not that Sandra has left me, or left us, and we are here forever; it is the fact that Sandra has gone before us. Without a personal life expectancy forecast we can be lulled into thinking that we are on this earth indefinitely as a world of relentless advertising would want us to believe. Yet, the thought of dying can in a bizarre way help us to live – live better!

In a sermon, *'Teach us to number our days'*,[72] which Robert Hamilton, an elder in Scrabo Hall, delivered during an evening service in 2017, he reminded the congregation of the verse, *'The days of our years are threescore years and ten; and if by reason of strength they be fourscore years. Yet is their strength labour and sorrow; for it is soon cut off and we fly away.'* [73]

Robert suggested that it might be helpful to compare the years of our lives to the days of the week. Hence, Sunday represents from birth to age 9; Monday – 10 to 19; Tuesday – 20 to 29 and so on. Using this illustration, Sandra lived 'until Friday morning', and by the same token, I am now – four and a half years later – commencing 'Friday afternoon'. Saturday midnight brings up threescore years and ten! Some may begin a second week, so to speak, and one or two may

---

[71] https://news.stanford.edu/2005/06/14/jobs-061505/
[72] Psalms 90:12 (KJV)
[73] Psalms 90:10 (KJV)

even experience a 'Bank Holiday Monday!' When thinking about life in this way we are confronted with the undeniable truth expressed by the Apostle James, *'For what is your life? It is even a vapour, that appeareth for a little time, and then vanisheth away.'* [74]

Christians are not exempt from illness or death, or indeed, irrespective of age, the suddenness of it at times. Neither are they exempt from losing a loved one, But oh, to think that a day will dawn when, thankfully, there will be no more pancreatic cancer – or any other horrible disease – because there will be *'no more death'*. [75]

Before the reality of all this is experienced, a great event must first take place as taught by the Apostle Paul in 1 Thessalonians – [76]

According to the Lord's word, we tell you that we who are still alive, who are left until the coming of the Lord, will certainly not precede those who have fallen asleep. For the Lord himself will come down from heaven, with a loud command, with the voice of the archangel and with the trumpet call of God, and the dead in Christ will rise first. After that, we who are still alive and are left will be caught up together with them in the clouds to meet the Lord in the air. And so we will be with the Lord forever. Therefore encourage one another with these words.

The truth of those verses is expressed in the following song –

There is a day,
That all creation's waiting for,
A day of freedom and liberation for the earth,
And on that day,
The Lord will come to meet His bride,
And when we see Him,
In an instant we'll be changed.

---

[74] James 4:14 (KJV)
[75] Revelation 21:4 (KJV)
[76] 1 Thessalonians 4:15-18

The trumpet sounds,
And the dead will then be raised,
By His power,
Never to perish again,
Once only flesh,
Now clothed with immortality,
Death has now been,
Swallowed up in victory.

We will meet Him in the air,
And then we will be like Him,
For we will see Him, as He is
One day!
Then all hurt and pain will cease,
And we'll be with Him forever,
And in His glory we will live,
One day! One day!

So lift your eyes,
To the things as yet unseen,
That will remain now,
For all eternity,
Though trouble's hard,
It's only momentary,
And it's achieving,
Our future glory. [77]

---

[77] https://genius.com/Lou-fellingham-there-is-a-day-lyrics

*'She was lovely and fair as
the rose of the summer.'* [78]

CHAPTER 11

Remembering Sandra

In her compelling poem, *'The Dash'*, [79] Linda Ellis writes of how important it is to take time to consider how we spend our *'dash'* –

I read of a man who stood to speak at the funeral of a friend. He referred to the dates on the tombstone from the beginning...to the end.

He noted that first came the date of birth and spoke of the following date with tears, but he said what mattered most of all was the dash between those years.

For that dash represents all the time that they spent alive on earth. And now only those who loved them know what that little line is worth.

For it matters not, how much we own, the cars...the house...the cash. What matters is how we live and love and how we spend our dash.

So, think about this long and hard. Are there things you'd like to change? For you never know how much time is left that can still be rearranged.

---

[78] https://en.wikipedia.org/wiki/The_Rose_of_Tralee_(song)
[79] www.thedashpoem.com

If we could just slow down enough to consider what's true and real and always try to understand the way other people feel.

And be less quick to anger and show appreciation more and love the people in our lives like we've never loved before.

If we treat each other with respect and more often wear a smile, remembering that this special dash might only last a little while.

So, when your eulogy is being read, with your life's actions to rehash...would you be proud of the things they say about how you spent YOUR dash?

Sandra's headstone includes that all important *'dash'* –

CARSON

In Loving Memory Of

SANDRA CAROLINE

Darling Wife Of Gary

And Devoted Mother Of Edward

17 May 1962 – 20 August 2014

Redeemed

Love's Last Gift… Remembrance

So, while the date of Sandra's death will always be remembered – as I know only too well – what really matters is the life that preceded it. That *'dash'* between Sandra's birth and the heartbreaking day just over four years ago is so difficult to quantify, but I am proud of the way my Sandra spent her *'dash'* and of the countless lives that she influenced for good.

Sandra often reminded me that Pastor Evans, a pastor in the Iron Hall when she was a child, said, "If you want praise, die!" Few will fail to grasp the significance of such a statement. There are, however, occasions when accolades given leave us wondering if the person spoken of is the really the person we knew! That, I'm quite sure, will not be the case as we remember Sandra.

Michael, a friend in my early days in the church at Ballyhackamore, once asked me if I knew the finest compliment one could receive in Heaven. Shaking my head to indicate that I didn't know, he suggested the answer should be – *'You haven't changed much!'* Amusing as that answer may be, it is not really in keeping with what the Apostle John teaches in one of his Epistles: *'Dear Friends, now we are children of God, and what we will be has not yet been made known. But we know that when Christ appears, we shall be like him, for we shall see him as he is.'* [80] That said, and without being prejudiced regarding my Sandra, I don't think she will have changed that much.

I can hear Sandra's unmistakable hearty laugh at the very thought of this chapter being included in this book. She was always uncomfortable receiving human praise in view of the teachings of the Lord Jesus in the renowned *Sermon on the Mount*. There, He highlighted the importance of doing things in secret and not for the purpose of seeking praise from others.[81] Sandra was concerned that praise on earth could result in not receiving it in Heaven in a future day.

I have no doubt that Sandra would have me make others aware of the awful nature of pancreatic cancer and I trust that the previous chapter, if not the book, will do just that. But this horrible disease must not be Sandra's legacy. I want her neighbours, those she met on holiday, her friends from church and elsewhere, her work colleagues, her schoolteacher, her hairdresser and even fellow patients and the nurses who so tenderly treated her at the Ulster Hospital, to have their say.

I think firstly of the void in the Rosehill neighbourhood where we had lived since marriage, and how it seemed genuinely affected by

---

[80] 1 John 3:2 (NIV)
[81] Matthew 6:1-6

Sandra's sudden and untimely death. She seemed to know just about everyone in the locality having held out a hand of friendship to so many of them.

Andrew lived just across the road and had grown up with Edward. His sympathy card reads, *'She was the sort of lady you could not stop and chat to without leaving with a smile on your face and feeling better about your day.'*

Rodney and Charlene lived in the house directly opposite and wrote, *'Sandra was one of the most open and friendly people we have ever met, and a true Christian example of one who was bubbling over with the joy of the Lord. Each one of you were blessed to have her as a wife, mother, daughter, sister, auntie and friend for she was beautiful inside and out. We will never forget Sandra. She was one in a million, and we will miss hearing her big laugh and her smiling face.'*

After Sandra died, I found that some neighbours struggled with knowing just what to say to me when we met. Again, I appreciate the words of C S Lewis when he wrote, *'I see people, as they approach me, trying to make up their minds whether they'll say something about it or not. I hate if they do, and if they don't.'* By and large, I found it more difficult when they didn't speak. Several notable incidents stand out when neighbours thankfully did stop to chat.

I recall one lengthy conversation with Dawn, who said, "I don't know what others will talk to you about, but I will always talk to you about Sandra." She then added, "Your Sandra never preached to me, but Christianity flowed out of her." When I think of those words, I am reminded of Edgar Guest's striking poem that I had occasionally quoted when speaking at meetings –

I'd rather see a sermon than hear one any day:
I'd rather one would walk with me than merely point the way.
The eye's a better pupil, and more willing than the ear,
Fine council is confusing, but example's always clear. [82]

---

[82] http://www.kubik.org/lighter/example.htm

One day while I was cutting the grass another neighbour approached me. I didn't know her name but remembered how Sandra had often waved to her from our car when we saw her out walking. Sandra had informed me that she lost a son in early life. Referring to Sandra, the lady calmly whispered in my ear with such sincerity, "She was a gift from God."

I think, too, of Valarie who lived just a few doors away, but who initially appeared rather shy when we first moved into the neighbourhood. Sandra boldly assured me, "I'm going to get to know her!" Not only did she get to know her, but she became her close friend, while her daughter, Rachel, became one of the most faithful attendees at the Ballyhackamore Sunday school. Valarie will miss Sandra.

Sometimes it was not words, but rather a gesture that typified the esteem in which Sandra was held. I think of Edward's friend, Jason, and his wife, Suzanne. Jason lived a mile or so away and we regularly took him to school. In more recent years we welcomed them both to our home for Sunday dinner. Their wreath, placed beside Edward and Anna's at the grave each Christmas, speaks volumes.

As my first Christmas without Sandra approached in 2014 I knew that I had to write to those folks whom Sandra had befriended during our holidays over the years. You see, Sandra built lasting friendships with strangers in a way that very few others could. Each year her Christmas card list grew longer, and yet, sending a card was never enough. She started writing her Christmas *letters* in November. I realised that I would have to write well before Christmas that year to tell them of Sandra's passing.

Their subsequent letters rekindled many memories as demonstrated by the one I received from Henna. In August 1988 we had travelled to Hanioti in Greece where Sandra befriended Henna, a lovely lady from the Netherlands. She then duly wrote to her every year. After writing, I received a three-page letter expressing her deep sympathy, and thinking about Sandra some 26 years earlier, stated. *'She lightened up the room in which she entered…it was always nice to receive a card written by Sandra for the Seasons with her humour and kindness.'*

One particular card arrived that first Christmas and in it the sender wrote of her desire to meet up with Sandra for a cup of coffee as they had missed each other during 2014. It was signed, 'Sylvia'. I wondered as to who Sylvia was before it dawned on me that she was one of Sandra's schoolteachers from Dundonald Girls High school with whom Sandra had maintained contact over all those years. Thankfully, her new address was written on the card and I realised that I needed to call and tell her that Sandra would never be able to have that cup of coffee.

A few days later I made my way up the path to Sylvia's home and rang the doorbell. Sylvia answered, and upon introducing myself, I was invited inside where I broke the dreadful news. How thankful I am for that treasured meeting when Sylvia shared her memories of Sandra's school days, and of how she delighted that Sandra was happily married. Then she said, "Your Sandra was just 'a one off'; beautiful on the inside and beautiful on the outside, a breath of fresh air in my class." As I left Sylvia's home that night, I couldn't help but think of the hundreds, if not thousands, of young girls she had taught throughout her career, and of how Sandra had stood out from the rest.

Sylvia's Christmas cards continue to arrive with their words of encouragement. On one card, she wrote, *'I think of Sandra too and what I will never forget is that infectious laugh she had. No one could ever be in Sandra's company and not be affected by her positive outlook, which I know she derived from her faith in Jesus. I have so many memories of her going back to when she was a teenager and they never fail to make me smile.'*

A friend from a local church wrote saying, *'I remember speaking to Sandra in McKee's Farm Shop just after a sad period in our life and she knew the right words to say. She gave me a hug, and I have never forgotten her empathy.'* Sandra had this unique ability to identify with the needs of others and listen in a way that led them to confide in her; sharing things that they hadn't shared with anyone else.

On the subject of hugs, I fondly recall an incident at the home of an elderly couple who had invited us for supper after I spoke at their church in Donaghadee one Sunday evening. As Sandra approached Bill to hug him with his wife Martha looking on, he joked that he believed that only his wife should be hugging him! Sandra spontaneously replied, "I don't care, you're getting a hug from me!" How very moving, when I received their sympathy card which read, *'We only heard last Sunday about your dear wife. Bill and I sat and cried. We loved to have you both in our home, and the happy memories we have of the good times we had. We could hardly wait for the next time to come.'* Sandra's hugs were instinctive and part of her DNA. Naturally, Edward and I were the main recipients of those hugs.

Jim, whose lovely wife Jackie had died that previous year, told me that his little daughter, Brooke, who ran enthusiastically over to Sandra after the Sunday morning services, simply said "I will miss her hugs." That was so very touching, coming with all the honesty and sincerity of a little child who was already grieving the loss of her mum.

Prior to one of my trips to Israel Sandra gave me a card that again demonstrated how much hugging meant to her. It sits prominently on the conservatory table and reads –

A hug can say 'I'll miss you'
or 'I'll be thinking of you',
It can say, 'You're someone special',
Or, best of all, 'I love you'.
It can sooth a hurt, or calm a fear,
Or cheer us when we're blue –
It almost seems a miracle
All the things a hug can do!

When the sun is refusing
to shine on your day
and you're finding it hard
just to cope.
When you're seeing more rain clouds
than stars in the sky
and you just feel like giving up hope;
That's the time when someone
comes along with a smile
and a warm hug
That says, 'It's okay –
Tomorrow is coming,
so don't give up now –
brighter moments
are soon on their way!'

Just a warm little hug
and a smile to cheer you,
To let you know now
that there's somebody near you
who cares.

To Gary…we love you so much…have a good time!

Sandra & Edward xxx.

While looking through Sandra's Bible, I came across a letter from Mrs Kennedy, an elderly saint who had written to Sandra just prior to Edward's birth in 1989. She wrote, *'…I thank the Lord for saving you and giving you such a lovely nature.'*

Pauline, one of our fellow Sunday school teachers wrote, *'Sorry it has taken me so long to send a card, but the truth is, I didn't know what to say. I am heartbroken for you and your family, but also for myself. I miss Sandra so much – for her care for our family, her sense of humour, her laugh and above all her warmth. Indeed a special person, as you and so many others have said.'*

Josephine was an outstanding Sunday school pupil back in the 1980s and 90s, and another memorable moment was meeting her while shopping one day near Holywood. She told me that she smiled every time she thought about Sandra, and added, "She had a beautiful heart."

Jennifer, a parent of two other exemplary Sunday school children, wrote, *'I will always remember her warm personality, smile and love for life.'*

Audrey, her dear friend since late teenage years, who thoroughly spoiled us both when we occasionally visited her and her husband Robert at their home in Balbriggan wrote, *'You have lost a wonderful wife and I have lost the most beautiful friend anyone could have.'*

Janet, who had got to know Sandra when her son went to the Model Primary School in Newtownards with Edward, wrote, *'Sandra was my beautiful friend who always made time for things that mattered. She laughed and made everyone laugh. I will miss her so much and I hope you have lots of memories – I know I do, she will never be forgotten.'*

One of the most touching messages came from Fiona, another friend from childhood days in the Iron Hall. She informed me that her son had asked her if he had ever met Sandra, and how she confidently replied, "No, because if you had you wouldn't have asked me!"

Leaving Scrabo Hall one Sunday evening, Clare simply said to me that it wasn't just that Sandra was special; it was the fact that *'she made you feel special.'*

Drew Craig wrote to me after speaking at Sandra's Thanksgiving Service and explained that the following day, when visiting the grave with his wife, he met *'a fully clad cyclist down on her knees'* who told him that she once had cancer also and had known Sandra for a lifetime. I knew immediately that it was one of Sandra's school friends— another Sandra. My Sandra had taken her to some of her own hospital appointments and sought to provide support during her own difficult times. I knew how keenly she, too, would miss Sandra.

A few months after Sandra's death I decided to leave a large quantity of her women's magazines at Hair Study. Shortly afterwards, her hairdresser (also called Sandra) wrote me saying, *'I looked forward to her coming into the salon as her personality lifted everyone's spirits, she always had everyone laughing with her infectious laugh. When she laughed the whole place laughed with her… I remember over a year ago I had talked her into joining the gym, so I walked in one day and she was on the cross trainer going backwards because she said it was easier, we couldn't breathe for laughing. All she talked about was "My Gary and Our Edward" which was so lovely to hear. I just want to say that I'm glad I knew such a caring, loving, bubbly, considerate person who always brightened my day. There's hardly a day goes by that I haven't thought of her.'*

Some of the most touching sentiments where expressed by those with whom Sandra worked during a lifetime in the travel industry – her managers, colleagues and customers.

One customer, Lucille, wrote of how she had built a great friendship with Sandra during her time at Clubworld, and said, *'I last spoke to her the week coming up to the 12th and she said she had been at the hospital the day before. She showed me photos on her phone of Edward's wedding and she was so proud. I want you to know it was a privilege to have known her and we could never forget the shock when we heard she was very ill… I went to the funeral and it was so so moving but what a tribute and testimony it was. We had planned to meet up but it wasn't meant to be. She was a delight to know…I can assure you the world is a sadder place without her in it.'*

Nan, a travel operator, wrote, *'Sandy was a joy to know, she touched everyone who met her. I will miss her so, so much.'*

John, one of Sandra's managers from Thomas Cook, had written to Sandra before calling to see her at the house on the evening before she took the stroke. He wrote, *'I don't know if you remember, but you always used to laugh at how I reacted awkwardly when you tried to give me a hug or cuddle when you felt I needed it. Still, I think you always understood, despite my embarrassment, how much I appreciated your caring, generous and considerate gestures, which perfectly sum up the lovely person that is you.'*

Delia, the owner of Clubworld Travel, penned these lovely words – *'Sandy was such a special person and such a wonderful work colleague. Always cheerful, always ready with a smile; her positive attitude was a real boon for everyone that worked with her. She was one of the most open and honest people it has been our privilege to meet.'*

A month after Sandra's death, Delia contacted me to say that a team of volunteers from the Northern Ireland travel trade was going to Oradea (a city in northwest Romania) in association with *Habitat for Humanity*. The volunteers would work in partnership with a local orphanage to build homes for those who were ready to live independently for the first time.

With little or no support from their families, expensive rent, and low wages, it would otherwise have been impossible for these young people to have a home of their own. This home would provide a firm foundation for a brighter future. It represented hope. Delia explained that she wanted to have a play swing erected in Sandra's memory and asked if I had a specific Bible verse that could be incorporated in the inscription. I suggested the last verse that Sandra had recorded in her personal Bible reading notes –

Have mercy on me, my God, have mercy on me, for in you I take refuge. I will take refuge in the shadow of your wings until the disaster has passed. [83]

---

[83] Psalm 57:1 (NIV)

A few weeks later I wept with pride when I received a text and photograph of a beautiful swing. Upon it were engraved the words –

IN MEMORY OF OUR DEAR FRIEND SANDY

REMEMBERED WITH LOVE
BY THE
NORTHERN IRELAND TRAVEL TRADE 2014
PSALM 57 V 1

Delia poignantly left an orchid on Sandra's desk at the Clubworld Travel shop. This was another one of those kind gestures that touched my heart. As previously mentioned, I had often sat at that desk waiting for her to file away paperwork before leaving for home. The NI Travel News magazines frequently sat on the counter and I recall reading the tribute to her colleague Trevor that had appeared in the June 2014 edition. Never for a moment did I imagine that the September/October 2014 edition would include a tribute to Sandra. But, how precious it was! It read –

There was a huge turnout in the Iron Hall Evangelical Church, East Belfast on Saturday for the funeral of Sandy Carson, one of the Province's best-known travel agents.

A packed congregation and crowds of mourners standing outside in Templemore Avenue heard tributes to Sandy who had worked in Clubworld Travel's Beersbridge Road, Belfast office, before being diagnosed with serious illness just a month ago.

Sandy has spent her whole working life in the Travel Trade, starting in Arcadia Travel in Belfast's Queen's Arcade as a teenager. From there she went to AA Travel in Great Victoria Street, then to Laser Travel, on to Knock Travel and then spent the biggest part of her travel career with Thomas Cook before joining Clubworld.

Sandy was an immensely popular work colleague whose sudden death shocked all who knew her. "Once when I was talking to her in the office she asked me to hold on for a wee minute and rushed outside to throw her arms round an elderly gentleman walking past the office. She explained to me, 'He comes up here very often, he's always on his own as his wife has just passed away and I just like to give him a big hug.' That was so typical of Sandy," said one mourner from the Trade who knew her well. *Sandy is survived by husband Gary and son Edward.*

Text messages from Sandra's work colleagues brought immense comfort as they expressed their deep affection for her. I think of Connie, who in her own inimitable way, sent a text message to Sandra's phone shortly after her death saying, '...*I'm also thankful for the Lord that he made you part of my life and I am truly blessed to have known you. If I can do half the kindness in my life as you did in yours I'll be happy. I love you Mrs C.'* I think also of Susan, her colleague in both Thomas Cook and Clubworld, and the poignant little ornaments she has left at Sandra's headstone.

It's startling to still think that while Sandra spent just four weeks in and out of the Ulster Hospital, she also lived on in the memories of fellow patients and the many angelic nurses who treated her as is evident from the following accounts.

Just a month after Sandra's death my own mum was taken into the Belfast City Hospital where she was diagnosed with dementia. Sandra and I had noticed the telltale signs for several years, and now it was confirmed. Sadly, she was unable to return home to be with my dad, so she was moved into residential care. As her memory deteriorated, I placed a framed photograph of her and Sandra on the unit beside her. It was taken on my mum and dad's 25th Wedding Anniversary and they looked so well together. Despite a fading memory, she recognised Sandra! Indeed, some three years later with an ever-decreasing recollection of others at times, she asked, "Were you married to Sandra? Did something happen to Sandra? Did Sandra have cancer of the pancreas? Sandra was lovely."

In October 2016 mum was admitted to Ward 5 of the Ulster Hospital before being moved to a care home more suited to her needs. Ironically, this was the very ward that Sandra had initially been admitted to on 20th July 2014. Consequently, the meeting to discuss my mum's transfer to her new accommodation was held in that same little office where Sandra and I had received the news of the pancreatic cancer diagnosis some two years earlier.

One evening while visiting mum in this ward, a nurse approached me to report that one of her colleagues had recognised me, but didn't know from where. I advised the nurse about Sandra having been admitted back in July 2014, and when she informed her colleague of this, she immediately made the connection. A couple of nights later the other nurse came over to me and said, "I'll never forget your wife – her smile and her faith." Over two years had gone by – and no doubt a multitude of patients – but Sandra had left a deep impression on this young nurse.

As I sat in Scrabo Hall one Sunday evening a year or so after Sandra's death, Donna made a point of sitting down beside me. Sandra and I had known Donna as one of the leaders when Edward attended their *Every Boys Rally* as a young boy. She was a beacon of light and a real inspiration after she too had been diagnosed with pancreatic cancer.

That evening Donna told me of her chemotherapy treatment, and of how another patient had approached her while receiving treatment at the Ulster Hospital and said, "You remind me so much of someone else who was diagnosed when I was here a year ago, but she died." Donna had then asked the woman if she remembered the other person's name to which she replied, "It was Sandra Carson." Donna wanted me to know that a year after meeting her very briefly, this fellow patient had not forgotten Sandra, or her bubbly spirit. That same spirit characterised Donna, who later also passed into the presence of her Lord after bearing her own illness with remarkable dignity.

Possibly the most precious sympathy card that I received was from Sarah; the nurse Sandra had taught in Sunday school, and who helped care for her during those last few days in the Ulster Hospital. She wrote, *'I feel privileged to have known Sandra; she was such a godly, yet down to earth, warm and kind person. I feel honoured that I had a small part to play in caring for her in her last days, and I'm truly sorry there was nothing more that I could have done. While Sandra was in (hospital) my mind was drawn to Psalm 121. I remembered learning in Sunday school. I said this one-day to Sandra, and she smiled and squeezed my hand. I pray that the words of it now would be of comfort to you. I pray that you would take comfort in the fact that God watched over Sandra from her first cry to her final breath. That he has protected her soul and that today she is with her Lord, free from all harm and all suffering forevermore. Death has been defeated…'*

Pancreatic cancer affected Sandra's body, but it never touched her heart or her soul. It did not have the power to rob Sandra of her peace and joy as she faced her diagnosis with extraordinary courage. It seems but right to give her the last word, so to speak. As I tidied Sandra's cookery books in the kitchen I came across two little *My Kitchen Prayer* notebooks. There were only a few pages left in each. In one page she had written the following poem taken from a bereavement card, the words of which surely reflect her love for our precious son Edward –

Of all the days throughout your life the saddest one has come, for life will never be the same without your loving mum. And though your heart is breaking, and it will for quite a while, remember all the love she gave, the radiance of her smile. A mother's love provides the rock you build your life upon, it stays with you forever and it helps you carry on.

In the other notebook were Sandra's handwritten words of a hymn expressing her trust and confident hope in her Saviour – [84]

---

[84] http://www.marmatt.com/music/songs/display.php?sn=but-i-long-to-see.txt

When my life on earth is finished,
and I cross the rolling tide.
And the beauty of the gloryland I see.
Many saints and friends and loved ones,
will be waiting there I know.
But I long to see the Christ who died for me.
Oh just think about the glory,
in the home beyond the sky.
Oh just think about the beauty,
we shall see by and by.
Many things on earth of value,
will be common over there,
but I long to see the Christ who died for me.

One of the many sympathy cards spoke of *'A life well lived... In loving memory of a Special Person.'*

Thinking of your loved one and remembering today, a life well lived that meant so much in each and every way…Filled with moments sweet and sad, with smiles and sometimes tears, with friendships formed and good times shared and laughter through the years…A life that leaves a legacy of joy and pride and pleasure, a loving, lasting memory our grateful hearts will treasure.

The sender added, *'Everyone who knew Sandra loved her… we feel blessed to have known her.'*

Each one of us can surely say, like those two Swedish schoolteachers who called at the Thomas Cook shop seeking help, ***'Thank God we met Sandy!'***

I thank God that I did.

To me you were someone special,
Someone set apart,
Your memory will live forever,
Engraved upon my heart.

*'Life is not about waiting for the storm to pass;
it is about learning to dance in the rain.'* [85]

CHAPTER 12

The Next Chapter

This chapter feels very much like an addendum. When I began writing on 23rd January 2017 I certainly had no intention of including a chapter with the word 'next' in it. Frankly, such a thought would have seemed absurd. At that time I concluded that 'living' had essentially ended – much earlier than I had expected. I only looked back. Yet now, some two years later, I find myself constrained to include it.

I had been privileged to visit the land of Israel during 2008 and 2010 and have the unspeakable joy of seeing many of those wonderful places that I often read about in the Bible: Jerusalem, Jericho, Nazareth, Capernaum and the Sea of Galilee to name but a few. Each experience challenged me, and my heart was thrilled as I used PowerPoint to show photographs of many of the amazing sites when I subsequently spoke in churches. I sought to declare that the gospel was not a fable – Christ was real and had walked here on this earth. Sandra enjoyed those presentations so much. Considering that she had not travelled with me during either trip, I promised her that we would go to Israel together some day. I had, therefore, little, if any, desire to return there without her.

Nevertheless, an opportunity arose unexpectedly to revisit Israel when Scrabo Hall announced a tour covering the dates 6th to 17th

---

[85] Vivian Greene. https://www.goodreads.com/quotes/132836-life-isn-t-about-waiting-for-the-storm-to-pass-it-s-about

May 2017 – with the latter date, ironically, being Sandra's birthday. But how could I accompany other Christians as they would excitedly walk in the footsteps of Jesus as I had previously done? I resisted any notion of going back and concluded that a trip to Israel was no longer for me. However, Edward and Anna had other ideas and routinely reminded me about it. They encouraged me to add my name to the rapidly expanding list of the folks who had signed up. I was bereft of enthusiasm though and felt that I would not be the best of company. The bottom line is that this holiday squarely fell into the 'enjoyment' category of life's events and as such lay well outside my new comfort zone.

Edward was determined though. So, as we sat at Sunday lunch on 29th January 2017, merely a few days after I commenced writing this book, he announced that following the morning service earlier that day he had told George Scott the Israel Tour speaker that his dad was going to go and would pay the deposit later. I was taken aback and wondered if he really had done so. Any doubts were erased that evening when George greeted me in the church foyer with his usual beaming smile. He expressed his delight at 'my decision' to join them. I hastily explained that while Edward had taken it upon himself to say what he did, I was still undecided. George, a brother with such an encouraging spirit, exhorted me to go, and so I assured him that I would think about it further. Obviously, I went home wondering what to do? I was now in a dilemma!

The NICS leave year finishes at the end of January, and as it happened, I had already decided to take my outstanding leave the following day, Monday, the 30th. I would have time to think about it and make a decision one way or the other. So, that morning, I mentioned it in prayer during my personal devotional time before heading up the Tullynagardy Road for one of my routine walks on what was a rather dismal winter's day. I had walked this road hundreds of times since Sandra's death, and while I greeted strangers, I strictly avoided lengthy conversations. These walks continued to afford a temporary escape from those around me.

That day was very different, though. A woman, whom I had never met before – or since – spoke to me as she walked along with her dog. She explained that she normally took the dog to the beach, but having broken her arm the preceding Friday, she was walking up the road that morning instead. The dog playfully gave me the stick it was carrying in its mouth, and as the minutes passed I judged that to go on ahead would have been rude, so, peculiarly, we walked along together.

I told this woman a little of my circumstances and my recent bereavement. Then, unexpectedly, 'Christine', as she introduced herself, began telling me of her 'pilgrimages' to Israel and of the places she had visited. I was amazed that of all the countries in the world, this woman was suddenly talking to me about Israel. I told her how that I, too, had been to that amazing Land a couple of times and that my son was actually encouraging me to travel there again with a group from his church. I emphasised that I had not yet decided. Understandably, I went home very much preoccupied with what had just happened.

After attending to a few things I visited the *Home Grown* vegetable shop In East Street on the other side of Newtownards. It had been one of Sandra's favourite shops, but one to which I had purposely not returned given my circumstances. As I entered the shop, George Scott immediately greeted me. He said that he rarely shopped there but had called in for a few apples after visiting someone nearby. I couldn't help but tell him about the stranger I had met with just a few hours earlier. George replied, "I think you are supposed to pay that deposit!"

Were these two surprise meetings on the same day merely fate. No, I believe these were further 'God-incidences' that convinced me that the Lord was telling me to revisit Israel. I duly completed the booking form later that day, and the following morning called at Aldor Travel, the company arranging the tour, to pay the deposit. As I considered the date, 31st January 2017, it was strange recalling that it was on that very day three years earlier, I had sat with Sandra at the open fire in the Culloden Hotel booking a cruise to Alaska.

After leaving work that evening I called at George's home and told him that I had booked. He said that he knew I would do so after having met him in the little vegetable shop. George had lost his lovely wife to cancer several years earlier. As we sat and talked for a few minutes, we both thought of how Sandra and Melba would each have given us their blessing. George had visited me faithfully during those early days without Sandra and frequently reminded me that 'God is good' no matter what the circumstances of our lives might be. The phrase, 'God is good' is repeated throughout the Scriptures. When King David had reminded the people of Israel of this marvellous truth, they replied, 'Amen'.[86] I confess that I often struggled to respond in this way during George's initial visits. Sadly, we are prone to only use this expression when things work out the way we want them to.

As the trip to Israel approached, I began telling others of the wonders of Israel, and soon Anna's parents, Alan, my friend from Ballyhackamore, and Bob, who had also recently lost his wife to cancer, all signed up. I could sense excitement building in others as the departure date approached. However, I personally still found it difficult to believe that I was going, much less, become enthusiastic about it. I was sure that I was supposed to go, but still felt a little bit like the Old Testament prophet, Jonah, who had been told to go to Nineveh despite having no great desire to do so. Nevertheless, as folk met together for pre-tour meetings to get to know one another, I gradually began to appreciate the fact that I was part of a special group, and that it was perhaps OK to look forward to going.

The 6th May 2017 finally dawned, and I was thankful to be travelling to the Belfast International Airport. The trip proved to be a milestone in my grieving experience as I found myself beginning to breathe again. I was with friends that I had known most of my life and with others that I would get to know, including several who had experienced heartache for a variety of reasons, including bereavement and divorce. I think of how Werner, a joint leader on the trip, and his wife Karin

---

[86] 1 Chronicles 16: 34-36

encouraged me. I am almost lost for words when I consider how their lovely young daughter, Caroline, was also diagnosed with pancreatic cancer a mere six months after we returned home. Thankfully, the diagnosis came early, and effective treatment was possible.

I shed many tears in Israel, but as the days passed, I also smiled and even occasionally laughed. How precious it was to realise that grief can coexist with other feelings. I had not laughed out loud since Matt and Rachel's wedding almost three years earlier on 10th June 2014.

The trip proved to be something of a spiritual reawakening too. The sights and sounds of this special place touched my heart anew as I walked through Zion, Gethsemane, the Garden Tomb in Jerusalem and the National Parks of En-Gedi, Timna, Bethshan and admired the views from the Fortress of Masada and the mountains of Carmel and Tabor, never mind the beauty of the Sea of Galilee and the nearby towns of Nazareth, Cana and Capernaum. So many memories came flooding back of those earlier visits to Israel when I had once been responsible for reading from God's word. I felt an urge to open my mouth again. So, when George asked if I would share a few thoughts from the Scriptures that first Sunday evening I, oddly enough, agreed. I had honestly never expected to be speaking publicly anywhere again.

I thought then of what George had spoken about earlier that afternoon when he had referred to the book of Ruth as we stood beholding Bethlehem's Shepherd's Fields. Several months prior to this I had read this short Old Testament book and felt a real affinity with, arguably, its key character, Naomi. Here was a woman who had travelled with her family to a new home in the foreign land of Moab where she tragically lost her husband and two sons within a very short period of time. She was a woman with a broken heart if ever there was one. As she mourned, Naomi decided it would be best for her to go back home to Bethlehem, but encouraged each of her daughters-in-law to stay behind in their homeland where they would perhaps find new husbands. She had concluded that she had nothing left to offer these two young women.

Eventually, Orphah agreed to stay in Moab, but Ruth was determined to go with her mother-in-law and would not turn back saying, *'Don't urge me to leave you or to turn back from you. Where you go I will go, and where you stay I will stay. Your people will be my people and your God my God.'* [87]

It was, however, Naomi's mindset that had struck me. She was convinced that she had nothing left to give. The author of that book explains how things, thankfully, did change for Naomi and her family, but during the depths of her grief, she hadn't envisaged such a thing. So, that evening, I took the opportunity to tell the rest of the group how I had been in a similar state of mind since Sandra's death with 'nothing left to offer'. At that point I was wondering if my life could still have meaning. Surprisingly, as we continued to meet together each evening, the desire to read stirred within me again and I had the privilege of sharing one or two further thoughts from God's Word. How peculiar after years of silence!

One of the most emotional experiences during the entire 11 days in Israel was walking through Hezekiah's remarkable tunnel in Jerusalem for the very first time. The Bible records that prior to the Assyrian invasion of Judah in 701 BCE, King Hezekiah built a tunnel under the city of David to bring the waters of the Gihon Spring to the southwestern side of the city. It took us 34 minutes to walk through this dark confined space with water covering our feet, and in parts, reaching our knees. We finally came out into the light and walked past the Pool of Siloam, renowned for the story of the healing of the blind man in John 9. For me, this walk seemed more than just a physical experience. I was beginning to see a glimmer of light in my life again after having spent so long in a dark, desolate place.

Family and friends detected a change when I returned home. Leaving an evening meeting in Scrabo Hall, my niece, Naomi, in her own distinctive way, said that she had seen my teeth for the first time in

---

[87] Ruth 1:16 (NIV)

almost three years! I can't help but think of a remark Sandra evidently made to my sister, Hilary, while she sat close to her in the hospital bed, shortly after the diagnosis. Referring to me as I sat stony faced on the floor, Sandra had whispered, "I don't like to see him looking like that." I realised at that point that Sandra would have been glad to see me smile again.

Back in Israel George had also invited me to 'give thanks for the bread' at the communion service in the Garden Tomb. In agreeing to do this I was very conscious that I was, in effect, making a personal commitment to continue 'breaking bread' upon my return to Northern Ireland. This couldn't be a one off. Sadly, I had not attended such a service since that awful Sunday in July 2014 when I had rushed home to take Sandra to the out of hour's surgery at Ards Hospital. How precious it was to once again partake of the emblems, bread and wine, which speak so vividly of the Lord's sufferings upon the cross, and to presently do so each Sunday morning at Scrabo Hall. How precious also, to occasionally pray publically at other meetings – something I also never anticipated doing again.

I am blessed to be feeling a little more like Edward's dad again. Edward had lost his mum, and in so many ways, I suspect, his dad. I still struggle with the thought that he no longer has his mum to also advise and guide him, but take comfort in knowing that Sandra saw him develop into the man that he is today, and in knowing that he is blessed with a good wife whom his mum dearly loved.

Has grief passed then you may ask? No, nor would I ever want it to. As I see it, grief never ends; it changes. I visit Sandra's grave every weekend and on the 20th of each month I take leave from work. However, I no longer dread the weekends coming. Because of a broken heart, I cannot ever be the Gary that I used to be, but with God's grace I trust that I will not be the Gary that I became during those initial years without Sandra. I'm slowly learning to accept that she would not want it to be any other way. I doubt if I will ever *'move on'*, but I do have a growing desire to *'live on'*.

I sometimes reflect on the sufferings of Job in the Old Testament and of how, in the blink of an eye, he lost his children, his wealth and his health. After everything that he endured, he said, *'Therefore, I despise myself and repent in dust and ashes.'* [88] What did Job mean by this? Was he confessing his sinfulness? The Hebrew word for *despise* can mean reject. The word *myself* doesn't appear at all in the Hebrew text. The Hebrew word for *repent* would indicate 'changing one's mind', while *dust and ashes* simply refers to mourning. Was Job then effectively saying, *'Therefore I reject and turn away from lamenting?'* I find that thought immensely challenging. There is certainly no doubt that Job's encounter with the Lord had given him firsthand experience of God when he says: *'My ears had heard of you but now my eyes have seen you.'* [89]

How thankful I am to be able to smile as well as cry. I dare, like Naomi in the book of Ruth, to see purpose in living before going to join my Sandra in that wonderful place which the Bible calls Heaven. That hope remains sure and steadfast.

I know who holds the future,
And He'll guide me with His hand,
With God things don't just happen,
Ev'rything by Him is planned,
So as I face tomorrow,
With its problems large and small,
I'll trust the God of miracles,
Give to Him my all. [90]

To quote C S Lewis for the final time: *'You can't go back and change the beginning, but you can start where you are and change the ending.'* [91]

---

[88] Job 42:6 (NIV)
[89] Job 42:5 (NIV)
[90] Alfred B. Smith (1916–2001)
[91] https://quotefancy.com/quote/781638/C-S-Lewis-You-can-t-go-back-and-change-the-beginning-but-you-can-start-where-you-are-and